Adapted from the book
EVEN THE VERY ELECT Will Be Deceived
By Karen E. Connell

Extended Life Christian Training Ministry

Normalizing Evil:

Through False Teaching

Karen E. Connell

NORMALIZING EVIL Through False Teaching

ISBN:13:978-1470095840
ISBN:147009584X
Copyright © 2012
Published by Extended Life Christian Training Center, Inc.,
Houghton, Michigan.

Permission is granted to photocopy all or parts of this book for distribution as long as it is done free of charge. However this book may not be reprinted or placed on the internet without express permission of the author.

Bible quotes are from several Bible versions. The particular Bible version is indicated by the following abbreviations.

KJV   The King James Version of the Bible. Published by Thomas Nelson Inc.

NKJV   The New King James Version of the Bible.

NIV   The Holy Bible, New International Version. Copyright 1973, 1978, 1984, by the International Bible Society.

NLT   New Living Translation Bible. Copyright THE LOCKMAN FOUNDATION,1960, 1962, 1963, 1968, 1971, 1973, 1975, 1977.

AMP   The Amplified Bible. Copyright by Zondervan Publishing House, 1965, Grand Rapids, Michigan.

Word studies and definitions are from several sources.
The particular source is indicated by the following abbreviations.

STR   Biblesoft's New Exhaustive Strong's Numbers and Concordance With Expanded Greek and Hebrew Dictionary. Copyright © 1994 Biblesoft & International Bible Translators, Inc.

THAY   Thayer's Greek Lexicon (Complete and Abridged Formats) Electronic Database. Copyright © 2000 by Biblesoft and International BibleTranslators, Inc.

B/D/B   Brown-Driver &Briggs Hebrew Lexicon, Copyright © 1993Woodside Bible Fellowship, Ontario, Canada, Licensed from the Institute for Creation research

CWSD   The Complete Word Studies Dictionary: AMG Publishers, 2003. Electronic Database Copyright © 1998, 2003 by Biblesoft.

DEDICATION

This book is dedicated to all those who are serious about becoming trained and equipped in order to do the work of their ministry

AUTHOR'S NOTE

I have been a serious student of God's word for over 40 years. During this time I have studied the King James Version as my preferred version of the Bible. I believe it to be the most reliable translation available. This is the version I also use for Scripture memorization. Since the Bible was not written in English, I make it a point to study Bible texts according to their original meanings as they were written in the Hebrew and Greek. I do however; use a variety of Bible translations in my writing and teaching ministries, in order to emphasize a Scriptural truth I am trying to relate. There is no way one single English translation can convey the depth of God's truth contained in the original Greek and Hebrew word meanings. Readers often miss the full impact of truth found in familiar verses of Scripture because they are used to hearing a verse the same way every time it is read or quoted. I have often thought I understood all there was to know about a certain verse until I heard it rendered in a different way, or checked it out in the original languages. In any case the Holy Spirit is our teacher. I have read certain verses in various translations and heard the Holy Spirit say "looks this up in the original" Hebrew or Greek only to be amazed at how much God had to say!

My intent then, for using various Bible translations is to make clear a truth I am conveying from God's word. For the same reason I do not always quote an entire verse, but focus on the phrase that is making my point. Jesus and the Apostles often quoted only a portion of an Old Testament Scripture to make their point. We must also remember that verse divisions and numbers were not added to Bible translations until around 1560 A.D.

Table of Contents

Authors Note 3
Introduction 7

Chapter 1—Normalizing Evil 10

Chapter 2—Calling Evil Good 15
    Sowing Seed for Financial Blessing 16

Chapter 3—Taking Captive the Souls of Men 20
    Jezebel the Spirit Over False Doctrines 21
    Word of Faith Doctrines 25
    The Prosperity Gospel 30

Chapter 4—Prosperity, Dominionism and World Transformation ... 36
    Kingdom Now World Transformation 36
    The Authority of the Believer 45
    Demonstrating the Kingdom of God 50
    The Seven Mountains Doctrine 54
    Conclusion 65

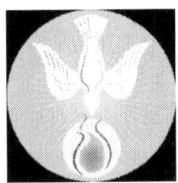

APPRECIATION

I am blessed and thankful for all those who have encouraged me to continue sharing the word of God with all who have ears to hear what the Spirit is saying to His Church in these end times. I am so grateful to my beloved husband Garry, who especially encourages me with his enduring love and his devoted servant's heart. I would also like to express my heartfelt appreciation to our co-laborer Martin Roos for his faithfulness and labor of love with the tedious task of proof reading.

"And God saw the light, that it was good: and God divided the light from the darkness."

Genesis 1:4

INTRODUCTION

This booklet has been written due to the great concern of many Christians, I included, who are seeing grave *deception* infect the body of Christ—and seemingly go unchallenged. There are popular and influential Christian networks and very prominent and powerful organizations that are embracing the "doctrines of demons," and the work of "seducing spirits" which we have been warned about in these end-times.

> *Now the Spirit expressly says that in latter times some will depart from the faith, giving heed to deceiving spirits and doctrines of demons* (1 Tim 4:1, NKJV).

False teaching is like *leaven* which if not purged from among us will end up spoiling the *whole lump.* No person or church is immune from experiencing Satan's counterfeit works and doctrines. God's Word tells us that he has the ability to appear as the genuine or real thing. Far too many Christians, I am sad to say cannot recognize Satan's deceptions and counterfeits—mainly because they are <u>very subtle</u> (barely detectable).

> "<u>*False apostles*</u> *have fooled you by disguising themselves as apostles of Christ. But I am not surprised! Even Satan can disguise himself as an angel of light. So it is no wonder his servants can also do it by pretending to be godly ministers. In*

the end they will get every bit of punishment their wicked deeds deserve" (2 Cor 11:13-15, NLT).

The tide of deception is rising quickly! Many of God's people are being fooled. Therefore, it is essential to increase and establish the importance of the watchman's ministry. We must allow watchmen to rise up and do what God has ordained them to do—which is to *clearly see the work of the enemy* and *use the "Sword of the Lord"* which exposes and destroys the works of darkness.

"Go, set a watchman, Let him declare what he sees" (Isa 21:6, NKJV).

God is appointing watchmen in these last days to watch over His people. Any minister or ministry that does not heed the warnings of God's appointed watchman will be in grave danger, because they will be the most vulnerable to Satan's counterfeits and deceptions—which are the earmarks of the last days before the return of Jesus Christ.

"But the end of all things is at hand; therefore be serious and watchful in your prayers" (1 Peter 4:7, NKJV).

But to simply accept the watchmen's ministry is not easy for many Christians. This ministry is often misunderstood and not always popular because watchmen are called by God *to deliberately look for problems* created by the enemy. When ministries or ministers believe they have an acceptable outward image to maintain—they will feel threatened and allow pride to rise up to defend themselves and their ministries and also attack the messages or messengers of God. As a result watchmen are often accused of being *divisive troublemakers* when they are in fact *troubleshooters* in God's kingdom. God makes them experts in watching for trouble and in identifying its cause and source.

The prophet is a watchman for my God over Israel ... He faces hostility even in the house of God (Hos 9:8, NLT).

As a prophetic teacher and watchman for almost thirty years I have experienced much opposition and misunderstanding. Howbeit, I must sound the alarm at the times God instructs me to do so. This is one of those times.

I pray those who *have ears to hear,* regarding what I am seeing as dangerous deceptions which are affecting God's people—will give careful consideration to the words written in this booklet. It may save the reader from being among those Jesus warned us about...

> ***For false christs*** (false anointed ones) ***and false prophets will rise and show great signs and wonders to deceive, if possible, even the elect*** (Matthew 24:24, NKJV).

Chapter 1

Normalizing Evil

In those days flocks will feed among the ruins... Destruction is certain for those who say that evil is good and good is evil; that dark is light and light is dark; that bitter is sweet and sweet is bitter (Isa 5:17, 20, NLT).

The Lord recently spoke the phrase *"the normalization of evil"* into my spirit as I was meditating on how "evil" is viewed as "normal" by the majority of people in the world today. For example, is it not evil to have sexual relations without being married? Yet according to the latest statistics by the Center for Disease Control, the overall percent of all births to unmarried women is around 41.0% which is up from 28 per cent in 1990... and in the black community it was over 75%! I knew the percentage rate was high, but this was way beyond what I had figured.

One of my biggest surprises was a December 2009 study, I came across that was conducted by the *National Campaign to Prevent Teen and Unplanned Pregnancy*, which included information on sexual activity. They found that... **80 percent of <u>unmarried evangelical young adults (ages 18 to 29) said that they have had sex!</u> Why is** this? Secular experts say the **"social stigma"** against out-of-wedlock births <u>has subsided</u>—giving way to a greater emphasis on stable longer term relationships—married or not!

My question is how has it become possible for the majority of professing young adult Christians to engage in sinful sexual activity—at a rate not much different that of non-Christians? It is simply because the STIGMA of SIN is no longer felt in our society, and even worse—within the majority of professing Christian circles. We don't want to judge sin as sin any longer—we especially don't want to see it as **exceedingly sinful** (Rom 7:13)—after all this may make people "feel bad" about themselves! When we stop using the Bible as our gauge for determining right from wrong and good from evil—it becomes quite common (normal) for people in just about every society to embrace all kinds of EVIL beliefs which leads to every imaginable EVIL behavior. Human beings are not to determine for themselves what is right or wrong, or good from evil (as Adam and Eve found out). Unless we yield to the authority that God alone gives to those He appoints as our leaders and teachers, to establish His ways and will by instructing us in His word, God's people will be ruled by *self-determination*, and this will always lead them into evil and deception, just as it did the nation of Israel.

> *In those days Israel had no king,* <u>**so the people did whatever seemed right in their own eyes**</u> (Judges 17:6, NLT).

When we adopt the attitude that no one has the right to "judge us" because we must decide for ourselves if something is good or right for us, we become a god unto ourselves and follow the evil dictates of our deceitful hearts and engage in evil ways which this world calls *normal*. However what the world calls *normal* God says only leads to death...

> *'As I live,'* says the Lord GOD,*'I* **have no pleasure in the death of the wicked,** *but that the wicked turn from his way and live.* <u>**Turn, turn from your**</u>

evil ways! *O people of Israel! Why should you die?* (Ezek 33:11, NKJV)

God is even now—pleading with those who practice sin and have embraced deception to turn from their evil ways—because they are **dead men walking!** God is righteous and must judge sin. God is releasing His righteous judgments with the desire they will cause people to turn away from what is evil and turn back to Him and live according to His ways. The above verse is not just talking about pagan sinners but it is addressing those who are part of God's Holy Nation (Israel—the church). He goes on to say...

*I say, when **righteous people** turn to evil,* **they will die...** *But if wicked people turn from their wickedness and do what is just and right, they will live* (Ezek 33:18-19, NLT).

There are a myriad of examples that one could give to demonstrate how evil has become the *normal standard* in many areas of our modern day culture and society. What God calls "evil" is now more often than not embraced as "good". For instance the "two parent" family with the "Leave it to Beaver" way of life, as depicted in the well-known 1950's American sitcom by the same name—is no longer the model for this generation. Ward and June Cleaver, the parents in that 1950's TV show, were the model parents which that generation of young people was given. This model has now been replaced with "same sex marriages or the "single parent" model, which God calls EVIL!

Many of this generation's heroes and leaders are immoral people who think nothing of flaunting their homosexuality or lesbianism as "alternative lifestyles" as models for our young people to emulate. The fashion industry has *normalized evil* by creating fashions that are seductive and immodest to say the least. Even professing Christian women find it *normal* to walk around dressed in tight fitting clothes that emulate that of "street walkers" by wearing clothing that looks to be painted on because they are so tight fitting. Christian women who should be role models for modesty think nothing of wearing miniskirts and shorts that cause the opposite sex to look and lust! O what shame we are bringing to God's HOLY name! Godly heroes are fast disappearing form the scene, and even young people being raised in Christian homes are looking to emulate the ungodly ways and lifestyles of the rock stars, movie stars and athletes, because it seems *normal* to do so.

> *The godly people in the land are my true heroes! I take pleasure in them!* (Ps 16:3, NLT).

These EVIL alternatives to God's heroes of faith and godly values are undermining the very foundation of humanity, as well as undermining of the foundation of the church. The true church of Jesus Christ has few godly role models for this next generation to look up to. Well known ministers are being exposed as homosexuals, adulterers, liars and cheats. What's even worse is the fact that more and more of our Christian mainline denominations, which once upheld God's standard for holy living, are now sanctioning these EVIL alternatives. They have even gone so far as to *ordain* homosexuals and lesbians as their ministers, rather than upholding the standard for holiness and the true Gospel which has the power to deliver these poor souls from the bondage of their sin. God is not pleased that His people are ignoring or justifying what is evil, and accepting it as a *normal* way of life. People think God "understands" and overlooks our ways of thinking and behaving, but He does not!

> *"Therefore take heed to your spirit, That you do not deal treacherously"...You have wearied the LORD with your words; Yet you say, "In what way have we wearied Him?" In that you say, "Everyone who does evil Is good in the sight of the LORD ... "Behold, I send My messenger, And he will prepare the way before Me. And the Lord, whom you seek, Will suddenly come to His temple, Even the Messenger of the covenant, In whom you delight. Behold, He is coming," Says the LORD of hosts... "But who can endure the day of His coming? And who can stand when He appears? For He is like a refiner's fire And like launderers' soap... He will sit as a refiner and a purifier of silver; He will purify the sons of Levi, And purge them as gold and silver, That they may offer to the LORD An offering in righteousness... "Then the offering of Judah and Jerusalem Will be pleasant to the LORD, As in the days of old, As*

> *in former years... And I will come near you for judgment; I will be a swift witness* <u>**Against sorcerers, Against adulterers, Against liars, Against those who exploit wage earners... — Because they do not fear Me," Says the LORD of hosts**</u> (Mal 2:16-17; 3:1-5, NKJV).

In the above text God tells us he is sending his messenger to *prepare the way* for the advent of the Lord Jesus. This messenger represents John the Baptist, who prepared the way for the ushering in of the kingdom of God which came through the ministry of Jesus Christ. The message of repentance is again preparing the way for the second advent of Jesus. John the Baptist was also represented by Elijah—because his preaching of repentance led to the confronting of sin in the lives of leaders like Herod. And just as Elijah confronted the *false prophets* so too these messengers of repentance will likewise confront these same issues in the church today.

The message that these "John the Baptist" type ministers bring, is one of repentance and holiness. God is bringing an awakening to sin and deception through these messengers and causing many to be awakened to the **fear of the Lord**. The deception of sin and the evil keeps on growing by leaps and bounds, so that the church is in grave danger! Is it any wonder God's Word tells us ...

> *Unless those days* (the end times) ***were shortened, no flesh would be saved; but for the elect's sake those days will be shortened... For...if it were possible, they*** (all that is false and evil) ***shall deceive the very elect*** (Matt 24:22, 24 NKJV, parenthesis mine). [1]

---

[1] For an in depth study on the subject of how and why God's people are being deceived see the author's book *"IF POSSIBLE Even the Very Elect Will be Deceived"* which can be obtained by going to the resource page at www.extendedlife.com

Chapter 2

Calling Evil Good

Of course it is easy to expose sin that is obvious such as sexual immorality, murder or stealing. I hope that no professing Christian would try to deny these things as being sinful. However, what about sin that "looks good" because it <u>seems</u> to be "helping people" and making their lives "better?" This type of sin comes in the form of "error" or false teaching that is masked by "good works." Because of this the line between "good" and "evil" is being blurred for many Christians. As a result <u>mixture</u>—<u>compromise</u>—<u>confusion</u> have invaded the lives of Christians and their churches, so they are no longer able to discern "good" from "evil" and effectively preach repentance from sin and share the true gospel of the kingdom with sinners.

I was recently sent a video clip of a documentary made by a secular news reporter from Nigeria. I watched this clip which greatly disturbed and saddened me. This video revealed how "evil" doctrines of demons, which many American "Christian" leaders—deem to be GOOD, have spread into third world countries. These teachings so widely accepted as GOOD are in fact EVIL and continue to infect millions of Christian leaders and professing Christians worldwide with their grave deceptions. The false doctrine in the clip I viewed is a very familiar doctrine to multitudes of Christians which says: [2]

> *God wants His people to prosper financially and the way to receive God's blessings of prosperity is by sowing seed* (money) *into good ground* (i.e. a good ministry).

Sowing Seed for Financial Blessings

Sound familiar? This false teaching known as "sowing seed" in exchange for God's blessing of *prosperity* has shipwrecked the faith and the lives of so many in the body of Christ around the world. My husband and I "sowed a lot of seed" into prosperity preaching ministries throughout the years. It shames me to admit our motive for the most part was that of "greed"—which has been *redefined* by this false doctrine as the desire to "prosper" which in turn means to receive God's **financial and material blessings.** We were awakened to this deception—but only by a series of very painful judgments which God sent into our lives, without which our eyes would never have been opened to the truth from His word concerning this false "faith for prosperity" doctrine.

First of all, this false teaching revolves around two key Scriptures. One that is usually quoted is something Jesus said:

> **Give, and it will be given to you***: good measure, pressed down, shaken together, and running over will be put into your bosom. For with the same measure that you use, it will be measured back to you"* (Luke 6:38, NKJV).

---

[2] To view this video go to www.johnthebaptisttv.com to see the video *"Nigeria's Millionaire Preachers."* (no, this site is not put out by the "Baptist "denomination). Founder Andrew Strom is also what I term a watchman prophet. I highly recommend his book *"Kundalini Warning"* which *exposes false spirits invading the Church.*

In essence, this false teaching says the more "seed" (money) you sow—the more you will get back from God! If you give a teaspoon full—you will receive a teaspoon full back, or if you give a truck load you will get a truck load back! We must remember that CONTENT taken out of CONTEXT is a PRETEXT (false premise). All false doctrines are based upon either no Scriptural proof or Scriptures being taken out of their context in order to support false ideas. For example the **context** for (Luke 6:38) is referring to the "giving" and "receiving" of *condemnation* or *forgiveness* according to the measure we use to mete these out. The context has nothing to do with giving and receiving money! What this text actually tells us is—if we give judgmental criticism it will be given back to us with the same measure with which we give it—and the same holds true for the giving and receiving of forgiveness as well.

Another example of Scriptures being taken out of context, in order to manipulate people into giving money into the ministries of false leaders, is the misuse of the **parable of the sower** (Matt 13:4-9, 19-23). This parable is used to falsely teach how one can get a **bigger return** (30—60—100 fold) on their investment of "sowing of seed" (money) into the kingdom of God. Those who teach this idea of sowing seed, say we must sow it into **good ground**. Of course those who teach this want people to perceive their ministry as "good ground" because of how "prosperous looking" it appears to be—all because of using this false premise for prosperity. Behind all of this however, is the sin of greed (idolatry) both on the part of the "givers" and the "receivers" who embrace this doctrine of demons.

This parable again has *nothing* to do with MONEY—rather the seed represents the WORD of God (Matt 13:19) and the CROP mentioned, which can yield a hundred—sixty—or thirty fold, is not a crop of *money,* but a crop of *faith* that *comes from hearing the word* (seed sown). The Bible clearly teaches that *"faith comes by hearing the* (sown in us—rhema) *word from God"* (Rom 10:17). Jesus even ends the telling of this parable by saying ... *He who has ears to hear,* **let him hear** (i.e. receive rhema "seed") (Matt 13:9).

There are now many ministers who once knew the truth, but have gotten their eyes on "money" and "power" and their lust for these things have turned them from the narrow road—on to the broad road of destruction. They promise much—but deliver nothing of eternal value.

> *These false teachers...laugh at the terrifying powers they know so little about, and they will be destroyed along with them... Their destruction is their reward for the harm they have done... <u>They commit adultery with their eyes, and their lust is never satisfied</u>. They make a game of luring unstable people into sin. They train themselves to be greedy; they are doomed and cursed... They have wandered off the right road and followed the way of Balaam son of Beor, who loved to earn money by doing wrong... These people are as useless as dried-up springs of water or as clouds blown away by the wind — <u>promising much and delivering nothing</u>. They are doomed to blackest darkness... They brag about themselves with empty, foolish boasting. With lustful desire as their bait, they lure back into sin those who have just escaped from such wicked living... They promise freedom, but they themselves are slaves to sin and corruption... when people escape from the wicked ways of the world by learning about our Lord and Savior Jesus Christ and then get tangled up with sin and become its slave again, they are worse off than before... It would be better if they had never known the right way to live than to know it and then reject the holy commandments that were given to them.* (2 Peter 2:12-15, 17-21, NLT).

I pray what I am about share in the remaining pages of this booklet will be carefully considered by all who read on. I especially pray that these things will be considered and understood by those who may be listening to or possibly embracing some of the false teachings that are mentioned and will be expounded upon. These false teachings are what very nearly destroyed my life and my husband Garry's life, because we once embraced these things. It was only through the grace and mercy of our Lord that His revelation and insight was given to us to free us from our captivity to Satan's deceptions. It was because of our release from the error we held that the deliverance and watchman's ministry was given to us by God. These false teachings produce immense strongholds by the demonic realm, which involve a great many deliverance issues. If what I am discussing is something new to you, then possibly you will be forewarned and not fall prey to these things should you run across them at some time in the future. Therefore I pray the light of God's Word will reveal to you the truth and any error you may have embraced.

Because God *extended* His mercy to us and gave us His *life* which delivered and restored to us a right relationship with Him and with each other (for our marriage was also in ruins) we were given from God the name for this ministry—EXTENDED LIFE Christian Training Ministry. We were given the mandate to equip—train and repair the House of God (the church). Our ministry logo Scripture is...

> ***For we were bondmen; yet our God hath not forsaken us in our bondage, but hath extended mercy unto us... to give us a reviving, to set up the house of our God, and to repair the desolations thereof*** (Ezra 9:9, KJV).

Chapter 3

Taking Captive the Souls of Men

Those leaders who teach the false doctrines of "dominion now" and "prosperity" are being motivated by Satan's lust for **wealth, recognition** and **power**, and thereby misuse the Scriptures to justify these lusts. Satan's lust for power, wealth and recognition can be clearly seen by the three temptations he set before Jesus. These demonic desires are especially being promoted by those who teach the false doctrines being discussed here. It is most important to understand that Jesus did not fall prey to these lusts because He did not agree with or yield to Satan's "reasoning" to try and legitimize these temptations (Matt 4:3-11).[3] Satan tried to entice Jesus with *wealth, recognition* and *power* by tempting Him to …

- Use His ability to create needed resources (i.e. create bread)… to obtain illegitimate WEALTH (vs. 3).

---

[3] I personally have heard much clever "reasoning" attached to these false teachings which misuse Scriptures that can easily go undetected if one is not skilled in using the word of God as the foundation for what is being taught. I learned the hard way not to accept all that I hear, but to allow the Lord to reveal the truth through the Scriptures, which will expose all wrong teaching.

- Demonstrate God's power as a means of legitimizing his identity… to obtain illegitimate RECOGNITION (vs. 6)
- Take the kingdoms of this world from Satan before it was His time to do so… to obtain illegitimate POWER (vs. 8)

Had Jesus given in to Satan's temptations, Satan would have received from Jesus what he is now getting from those promoting and following the false teachings put forth in this study—which is WORSHIP (honoring Satan) through acts of SERVING (works that are pleasing to him). Jesus exposed Satan's agenda by using the word of God…

> *It is written, 'You shall <u>worship</u> the LORD your God, and <u>Him only you shall serve</u>'"* (Matt 4:10, NKJV).

If Satan can create the desire for *wealth, recognition* or *power* within us—we will ultimately end up serving or pleasing Satan when we give into his temptations to serve or please **ourselves—other people**—or **the kingdoms of this world.**

Professing Christians who are ignorant of what the Bible really teaches, or those who choose to ignore the Word, and pick and choose what is to *their liking* from it, will be easily enticed to lust after **power, wealth** or **recognition**, and will also eagerly drink in the intoxicating lies of doctrines of demons.

> *For the time will come when they will not endure sound doctrine, but according to <u>their own desires</u>, because they have itching ears, they will heap up for themselves teachers; and they will turn their ears away from the truth, and be turned aside to fables* (2 Tim 4:3-4 NKJV).

Jezebel…the Spirit over false doctrines

The "face of Christianity" for multitudes has been changed from that of a HOLY BRIDE—to that of the idolatrous "face of Jezebel," the harlot spirit of **greed**. There are those who wonder how the Jezebel spirit is given the right to enter and influence Christian lives, ministries and churches. The Bible reveals that this spirit operates through a *counterfeit prophetic anointing* which is empowered by false teachings when embraced, release seducing spirits that bewitch God's people.

> *Notwithstanding I have a few things against thee, because you allow that woman Jezebel, which calls herself a prophetess,* **to teach and to seduce** *my servants...* (Rev 2:20, NKJV).

Jesus addressed the above statement to the church in Thyatira that had allowed the *Jezebel spirit* to operate. This city was a thriving commercial business center, where wealth and social success was promoted through the pagan culture. When you read about Jezebel, King Ahab's wife in the Old Testament, you can clearly see her connection to *greed*. Therefore, the false teaching promoted by this counterfeit prophetic spirit is associated with *greed* for wealth—prosperity—social success. These things were being used to seduce God's people in the church of Thyatira through false teaching coming from the Jezebel spirit that led them into *idolatry* and *perversion*.

Archaeologists have uncovered evidence of many trade unions in Thyatira and found that membership in these trade unions would have been necessary in order to prosper *financially* and *socially*. The trade unions were involved in ungodly cultural practices that involved idolatry and loose morals.[4]

Trade unions are known for *negotiating*—in order to secure what is wanted by those they represent. As I read about Thyatira's trade unions, I couldn't help but think of the *negotiation tactics* that Queen Jezebel used in order to get what King Ahab wanted (1 Kings 21:1-16). The word *negotiate* is defined *as maneuvering through, around or over an obstacle to achieve success*.[5] If you are familiar with the account of how Jezebel *negotiated* the obstacle of Naboth's refusal to give up his vineyard, you will remember that the *ungodly maneuvers* of lying and murder were used to achieve a successful outcome for Ahab. The sin of *greed* (which was Ahab's sin) will always open the door to the *maneuvers* of the Jezebel spirit. One way the Jezebel spirit is able to

---

[4] Nelson's Illustrated Bible Dictionary, © 1986, Thomas Nelson
[5] Collins English Dictionary - Complete & Unabridged 10th Edition 2009 © William Collins Sons & Co. Ltd. 1979, 1986 © HarperCollins

disguise itself is through operating in a counterfeit prophetic gift. Just because someone can "accurately" prophesy does not mean it is the Holy Spirit doing the prophesying. Even psychics can receive some very accurate information from unholy spirits. Therefore, undiscerning or greedy Christians can be easily seduced by this religious spirit.

False ministers promoting doctrines of demons are able to legitimize their ministries and false teachings through lying signs and wonders such as *personal prophecies*, or by *healings* and *miracles* of all kinds. Thus, Christians are deceived if they are unskilled in the word of God or ignore what the word says. They become deceived simply because a ministry looks "prosperous" (calling what is evil good) or because a ministry seemingly confirms what it teaches (even if it is false) through signs and wonders—which are in many cases, actually performed through the power of demonic spirits such as the Jezebel spirit. Thus those who are deceived by false doctrines fall prey to the power of divination—and end up calling what is EVIL—GOOD!

I hear God saying He is going to bring an escalation of His judgment and the exposure of false ministers and ministry organizations that **will not turn from their evil ways**. The following text is what God is saying at this time to those leaders who will not receive correction through the truth of God's word and turn from their wicked ways…

> *Will you* **hunt the souls** *of My people, and keep yourselves alive? …And will you profane Me among My people* **for handfuls of barley and for pieces of bread** (so you can make a living), *killing people who should not die, and keeping people alive who should not live, by your* <u>lying to My people who listen to lies?</u>" *…Therefore thus says the Lord GOD: "Behold, I am against your magic charms* <u>by which you hunt souls</u>*… I will tear them from your arms, and let the souls go, the souls you hunt like birds….* <u>I will also tear off your veils</u> (expose them) *and deliver My people out of your hand, and they shall no longer be as prey in your hand. Then you shall know that I am the LORD. .."Because* <u>with lies you have made the heart of the righteous sad,</u> *whom I*

> *have not made sad; and you have strengthened the hands of the wicked, so that he does not turn from his wicked way to save his life... Therefore* <u>**you shall no longer envision futility nor practice divination**</u>*; for I will deliver My people out of your hand, and you shall know that I am the LORD"* (Ezek 13:18-23, NKJV).

What struck me most as I watched the video from Nigeria, was that false prosperity teachers and preachers target people who are educated, and those who either have or are seeking money making careers—who have a desire to "go to a whole new level" with God (so they can realize **their desires** i.e. lusts). False ministers do not usually mingle among the poor, but prefer the "movers and the shakers"—who have the means to create wealth (and sow seed). How much "seed" can a sick, poverty stricken beggar sow? The Apostle Paul warned us of these wolves who masquerade as spiritual leaders.

> ***Elders* (leaders)** *must have a strong and steadfast belief in the trustworthy message he was taught; then he will be able to encourage others with* <u>**right teaching**</u> *and show those who oppose it where they are wrong ...For there are many who rebel against right teaching;* **they engage in** <u>**useless talk**</u> **and** <u>**deceive**</u> **people.** *This is especially true of those who insist on* <u>**circumcision for salvation**</u>*... They must be silenced. By their wrong teaching, they have already turned whole families away from the truth.* <u>**Such teachers only want your money**</u> (Titus 1:9-11, NLT).

Like the Pharisees, false religious leaders place an emphasis upon certain "works" like **sowing seed—tithing** and **giving offerings**. Other WORKS may also include things like making **positive confessions** or **quoting Scriptures** that promise to give us our hearts desires.

It is noteworthy that Jesus twice emphasized the "works" of the Christians in the church of Thyatira.

> *I know thy <u>**WORKS**</u>, and <u>charity</u>, and <u>service</u>, and <u>faith</u>, and thy <u>patience</u>, and thy <u>**WORKS**</u>; and <u>the last to be more than the first</u>* (Rev 2:19, KJV).

Jesus said he *knew* their <u>*works, charity* and *service*</u>. Some say He was commending this church for these things, but there is nothing in this text to confirm this. He simply says He is aware of these things. Why is this important? It is because false ministries and ministers often use their works—charity and service as a disguise. Jesus made this statement to the church in Thyatira because they were tolerating false teaching from a false prophetic minister which were being disguised by good looking works of—*charity*—and *service*, and *faith*, but these "works" were hiding the Jezebel spirit's evil agenda. God's Word makes it clear that He is aware of those who embrace *counterfeit prophetic* ministries and their greedy, motives and agendas. The prophet Ezekiel, who was a watchman prophet over God's people, had this to say:

> *Again a message came to me from the LORD: "Son of man, give the people of Israel this message: In the day of my indignation, you will become like an uncleared wilderness or a desert without rain...* <u>**Your prophets plot conspiracies**</u> *just as lions stalk their prey. They devour innocent people,* <u>**seizing treasures and extorting wealth**</u>*... Your priests have violated my laws and defiled my holy things. To them* <u>there is no difference between what is holy and what is not</u>*. And they do not teach my people the difference between what is clean and unclean...* <u>My holy name is greatly dishonored among them</u>*... Your leaders are like wolves, who tear apart their victims.* <u>They actually destroy people's lives for profit!</u> (Ezek 22:23-27, NLT).

Word of Faith Doctrines

It is interesting that when Jesus addressed the church in Thyatira He also said he was aware of their *faith* and *patience* which also produced *works*. In fact He goes on to say that these *last works* (of patience and faith) were more (greater) than *the first* (works of charity—service). Therefore, the works of FAITH and PATIENCE are the prominent issues mentioned by Jesus, concerning this church in which the Jezebel spirit was operating. The correlation between the popular *"Word of Faith"* movement, that also propagates the false "prosperity gospel" and what Jesus told this church is striking! The word *patience* used in (Rev 2:19) is the Greek word (Strong's 5281) *hupomone* (hoop-om-on-ay') which refers *to that quality of character which does not allow one to surrender to circumstances.*[6] The *Word of Faith* movement has largely been founded upon the text in (Mk 11:23-24) which they say teaches us that anyone who ...

> **does not doubt in his heart, but believes that those things he says will be done, he will have whatever he says... Therefore I say to you, whatever things you ask when you pray, believe that you receive them, and you will have them** NKJV.

This portion of Scripture has again been pulled out of its context in order to promote a false concept of *faith;* which in a nut shell teaches that *faith* is the product of *believing and speaking*. Therefore, they teach if you really *believe what you are saying—then you will have whatever you say!* Also *whatever you ask God for when you pray if you can believe for it without doubting—you will receive it."* As a result, "speaking and believing" become the keys to activating ones faith. It is also taught that "words can create"—just as God spoke things into existence—this means so can we because we are "like God" (because we are created in His image). Looking at the text quoted above, apart from its context, one could "reason" this to be true. However, the *content* of what Jesus said is the result of the *context* from which it comes. What Jesus stated in (Mk 11:23-24) was in relation to *three* things He was teaching at that time which are connected to having *genuine faith*. The three things Jesus taught within the context of (Mk 11:23-24) were:

- **The parable of the fig tree**... (Mk 11:12-14) The fig tree represents a professing believer who is <u>not fruitful</u> or having God's character (Gal 5:22-24). They look "good" but do not have genuine faith because there is... **no godly character** (fruit).

- **God's temple is a place of prayer**... (Mk 11:15-17) The temple was defiled because <u>merchandising</u> (making money—greed) was embraced and placed above prayer.

---

[6] The Complete Word Study Dictionary: New Testament © 1992 by AMG International, Inc. Revised Edition, 1993)

Prayer is not just making our requests known, but also hearing what God has on His heart regarding His agenda. What comes out of the temple of God should be (true communion with God) producing genuine faith— not a false faith that produces **greedy desires and petitions.**

- <u>**Unforgiveness issues**</u>… (Mk 11:25-26) Jesus said these must be dealt with, because "bitterness" that is being harbored by unforgiveness (is rebellion or witchcraft 1 Sam 15:23) and will give us Satan's lusts (fleshy desires) as stated in (JN 8:44). If we are not released from our sin… **false faith is produced by sin and witchcraft.**

Without taking into consideration the above three points, one's motives and attitudes go unchecked, when it comes to what we are "believing or asking God for." The kind of pseudo *faith* taught and demonstrated by those of the Word of Faith movement is founded solely upon believing in God, and believing what His word says (or what it is made to say by those who misuse it). Faith in God and His word *sounds good*, but the emphasis is on **believing** which is only *one aspect* of genuine faith. When you examine the word FAITH in its original meanings, you find there are *three aspects to faith* which must be present so that our faith will be genuine and not be lacking anything and end up becoming *a counterfeit faith*. The three aspects of faith found in the original word definitions mean to be [7] …

- **Convinced** …(believe it)
- **Yielded** …(Agree with it)
- **Obedient** …(act upon it)

Being taught that *believing* in God and in His word is all one needs in order to have genuine faith may sound good and reasonable— but it is not the whole truth of the matter. Satan and his demons believe in God and the word of God—but they certainly do not have *genuine*

---

[7] (Strong's 3982) from the root ***peitho*** (pi'-tho) Exhaustive Strong's Numbers and Concordance with Expanded Greek-Hebrew Dictionary. Copyright © 1994, 2003

complete faith in God or His word (Js 2:20).[8]

The Jezebel spirit teaches this false kind of faith. When addressing the church in Thyatira, Jesus made mention of their *faith* and *patience*. As previously stated the word **patience** referred *to that* **quality of character which does not allow one to surrender to circumstances**. When *believing* becomes the predominant aspect for *producing faith*—then what we believe becomes the foundation for our faith. According to the word of faith teachings <u>we must believe what we say will be done</u> because God is obligated to honor our words of faith—especially if you are "standing on the word." After all His word does say that **whatever things you ask when you pray, believe that you receive them, <u>and you will have them</u>**. However, what the word of faith teachings fail to make plain is that faith does not come by just *believing what we say* (even if we are quoting the word of God—which can be nothing more than an intellectual exercise). Real faith comes by **hearing** (receiving a personal revelation) because of what God *personally* reveals to our spirit as truth (which is the rhema word) from His written (logos word) (Rom 10:17). Many deceived Christians think because they know the word and can quote the word and the more they can do so—the greater their faith will be.

I remember sitting under a pastor many years ago, who was a word of faith preacher, that firmly believed we could **have whatever we say if we really believed what we were saying.** At one point this pastor's wife fell off a ladder and broke her arm. I saw it hanging like a broken twig as she cried out in pain. The Pastor prayed a *prayer of faith*, quoting a host of healing verses, in order to have faith for believing she was healed. He had refused to take her to the hospital, more out of fear than faith—because he had no medical insurance. He kept telling his poor wife to <u>say</u> over and over again … *"I believe my arm is healed—I am the healed of the Lord!"* He kept insisting that she was healed—because God was her healer… until the pain and swelling made it very clear she needed to go to the hospital for treatment.

This kind of <u>refusal to surrender to circumstances</u> or the display of a pseudo **"patience"** was not coming from genuine faith. It was however, the kind of *patience* I had seen displayed over and over again by many (myself included) who claimed to have faith for all kinds of

---

[8] The devil and his demons also believe and tremble.

things. Neither this Pastors wife nor the Pastor himself ever claimed to HEAR God tell them He was going to perform a miracle (which is what he was saying he was believing God for). Our BELIEF must come from what is directly from God to us by His Holy Spirit. No one present received a prophetic word—a word of knowledge or anything from God's written word that could be the foundation for the faith needed to see a miracle occur for his wife. Works such as...

- Positive confessions
- Quoting Scripture
- Faith declarations

All of these things become the <u>*dead* works</u> of a pseudo faith when we try to create faith so we can "receive" what we desire from God. This kind of false faith along with its "works" has reaped havoc in so many lives of those who sat under such teachings. This kind of faith is based upon what "we call good and evil" and not what we hear God say is good or evil. If it is unpleasant it must be evil and if it is pleasant and to our liking it must be good. When our faith is lacking the essential aspects of genuine faith we will fall into grave error and deception, which will rob us of our holiness before God. Without holiness no one can see things the way God does. We will not stand blameless before Him, for trying to conjure up pseudo faith to fulfill our own desires.

The Apostle Paul mentioned the importance of not *lacking* in anything that is needed to produce genuine faith.

> *We are... night and day praying exceedingly that we may see your face and* <u>**perfect what is lacking in your faith**</u>... *so that He may establish your hearts* <u>**blameless in holiness**</u> *before our God and Father at the coming of our Lord Jesus Christ with all His saints* (1 Thess 3:10, 13, NKJV).

As stated, faith that is false is reliant upon *dead works* such as confessing the word, or trying so speak things into existence and any other number of ways that are used to try and impress or manipulate God into giving us what we are "believing Him for." This includes "giving" or sowing money as seed as we have already mentioned. Giving offerings and tithes with the motive of "believing" we are going to "receive" what we ask for, has become a way for many professing Christians of getting God to "save" them from sickness—poverty, a bad marriage—or any other number of problems—even including the salvation of loved ones!

The Prosperity Gospel

I recall being in a meeting where a key leader in a prophetic movement gave a testimony as to how God had saved certain family members after he and his wife had sown a large amount of money into their *own ministry*! Of course an offering was immediately taken up for those who also wanted to see their loved ones saved by "sowing a seed" into that ministry. It was quite a sight! The people "danced" their way down the aisles of that church filling up buckets with their "seed" to a *"rocking"* song that was blaring out the words **"money cometh!"** These kinds of manipulations and occurrences are all part of the *normalizing of evil* that is invading modern Christianity.

This type of false "prosperity" and faith teaching became popular in the body of Christ during the early 1960's and has gradually invaded the body of Christ worldwide. These false doctrines and the ungodly behavior and practices they generate have given Christianity a "black eye!" It only takes a little "leaven" to spoil the whole body...

> *You ran well. Who hindered you from* **obeying the truth***? This persuasion does not come from Him who calls you...* **A little leaven leavens the whole lump***... I have confidence in you, in the Lord, that you will have no other mind; but he who troubles you* **shall bear his judgment***, whoever he is* (Gal 5:7-10, NKJV).

Churches are now run like worldly business corporations with "prosperous" looking leaders taking up positions of wealthy CEO's within their organizations. Christians worldwide are being taught that God wants His children to believe for and accumulate wealth, **so they can do great exploits for God in His kingdom**. The accumulation of wealth (financial blessings) is being used to *demonstrate the kingdom of God* and confirm the *gospel of the kingdom* (using the prosperity message) which they are told can transform lives, cities and nations. This sounds good, but it is becoming a snare to many who once followed the "simplicity" of Christ and are now following another "gospel" and being led by another "spirit" that is leading them into doing things the world's way in order to achieve success and influence; all the while believing this to be their God ordained "ministry" and destiny.

So many verses of Scripture are misused, twisted and pulled out context to convince Christians that God wants them to be **wealthy** and that He wants the transference **of wealth** from the hands of sinners into the hands of God's people; so they can establish the kingdom of God upon the earth. For instance one verse that is widely being used to support this (demonic) idea, says:

> *A good man leaves an inheritance to his children's children;* **the <u>wealth</u> of the sinner is <u>laid up</u> for the just.** (Pr 13:22).

I can't tell you how many times I heard the *later part* of this verse quoted by those who teach these things. The fact is if you study the *entire verse* you will find it is not saying there is to be the transference of wealth (money) from sinners to saints! First of all, the CONTEXT for this verse reveals that God is talking about a **good man** who leaves a **good** inheritance as a *generational blessing* for his children. The preceding (vs. 21) states that *a righteous man will be rewarded with* **good**. The word GOOD is the key to understanding (vs. 22). The word "good" is the Hebrew word (Strong's 2895) ***towb*** (tobe) which means *what is* **<u>right</u>** *and what is* **<u>best</u>** *(according to God's definition—not ours)*. It also means *pleasant, pleasing and prosperous*. Therefore, if a person is doing what is **right** and what is **best** according to God' standard, then they are viewed as pleasant and pleasing in God's sight. This means they are doing things according to God's ways and will and this will cause them **to be prosperous** (successful). God views success in terms of being able to live a **righteous life**—not according to how much money or possessions and popularity one can achieve. People who do not know God or honor Him are able to achieve *success* as humans view success; which is in terms of wealth, power and recognition—which again is how Satan defines success.

If you take the time to look at the *key word* meanings in (Pr 13:22) you will find that the word **WEALTH** is the Hebrew word (Strong's 2428) ***chayil*** (khah'-yil) which refers *to strength, abilities and resources*. The word **SINNER** (Strong's 1322) in the Hebrew text according to the CWSD— is not a "noun" (describing a person) but a "verb" that refers to *doing what is sinful*. The phrase **LAID UP** is the Hebrew word (Strong's 6845) *tsaphan* (tsaw-fan') which means to <u>protect</u>, *to lurk, to hide, to lay up or to store up*. In its literal context then the phrase the **wealth of the sinner**—is referring to, <u>**protection from**</u> **strength—abilities—resources—that lead the righteous into sin**. This is quite a different meaning than what false teachers teach from this verse! God is trying to "protect" us from the "wealth of sin(ners)" not lead us into it by putting it into our hands! The wealth of sinners is the *strength* of their sin—which is the use of one's own abilities to *store up resources*. Anything we can do without complete dependence upon God's abilities is pride—the most powerful of all sins.

> *'Not by might nor by power, but by My Spirit,'*
> *Says the LORD of hosts* (Zech 4:6, NKJV).

God warned Moses of this very thing. He told Moses that any "wealth" meaning… any **strength—abilities—resources**—that His people would possess, would be because He alone would be their source for these things. He warned them not to think it had anything to do with their ability to obtain them.

> *Who fed you in the wilderness with manna… that He might humble you and that He might test you, to do you good in the end — then you say in your heart,* <u>*'My power and the might of my hand have gained me this wealth'*</u> *…"And you shall remember the LORD your God, for* <u>*it is He who gives you power to get wealth,*</u> *that He may establish His covenant which He swore to your fathers, as it is this day.. Then it shall be, if you by any means forget the LORD your God, and follow other gods, and serve them and worship them, I testify against you this day that you shall surely perish* (Deut 8:16-19, NKJV).

How many Christians who started out simply believing that they were <u>not to depend upon</u> *their human abilities—personal strengths— and the worlds' resources* as the means for doing the work of the kingdom of God—are now believing just the opposite? Because of hearing and receiving these doctrines of demons multitudes are now convinced they need to "excel academically" or achieve success through the "business world" or in some other arena of life; in order to *prosper* and have the money and influence to become "agents of change" and create *positive changes* in their nations. Countless numbers of Christians are trusting in the *wealth of sinners* to be used to transform people and nations (all for God's glory of course). Oh what a deception this is! It is not God who is receiving the glory for any perceived changes, but people and organizations that are being called the "church."

I recently heard a key leader in the "transformation movement" give a testimony of how *their ministry* had "gone to war" and through the spiritual warfare of their ministry, a complete economic turnaround had occurred in their territory. Not one time was God given the glory for this economic turnaround! Their boasting was not in God, but in *their ability* to do spiritual warfare, and in *their authority to* bring down a ruling principality that was said to be over their territory. How it saddens me when I hear professing Christians eagerly take credit for possessing the power and spiritual authority to perform signs and wonders. They have no idea how far they have fallen into deception and how much they have taken on the nature of the "angel of light" who is behind their power hungry agendas.

When it comes to the subject of wealth the argument is given that we need *money* to do the work of the kingdom. Yes, money is a resource that is needed to accomplish things for God, but it is not something we depend on or seek after or look for ways in which to obtain wealth. If we seek God and His kingdom (righteousness—peace—joy) money or whatever we need will be the "added unto's" which God will provide. By the way, the ONLY work of the kingdom is that of saving souls from an eternity in hell—not changing for the better the quality of our lives or nations through taking over the kingdoms of this world. There is no way that we can honestly and sincerely find ways to *serve God*, which means to do what God's Word requires; when we are taught by false teachers to *serve money* (or do what obtaining wealth requires). The desire to obtain wealth will require our very soul!

> *"No one can serve two masters. For you will hate one and love the other, or be devoted to one and*

> *despise the other. You cannot serve both God and money* (Matt 6:24, NLT).

Jesus never taught any of these false concepts, regarding wealth and personal prosperity. He never "courted" the wealthy—He ministered to the poor and needy. It is much easier for a poor person, meaning one who lacks strength—abilities—or resources, to obey the command of Jesus to *forsake all* and follow Him, than it is for a person who possess great abilities, influence and wealth. The wealthy person has found a place of recognition—admiration and independence, apart from God, all of which must be abandoned in order to follow Christ.

> *"Assuredly, I say to you that it is hard for a rich man to enter the kingdom of heaven. And again I say to you, it is easier for a camel to go through the eye of a needle than for a rich man to enter the kingdom of God"* (Matt 19:23-24, NKJV).

The Bible teaches that **the pursuit of wealth** is a <u>snare</u> no matter how good sounding the motive may be for pursuing it! It must be remembered that *any desire for money* <u>requires a love for money</u>. We desire what we love—and we love what we desire. Therefore God must be the desire of our hearts for He alone is our answer and the source for everything…not money!

> *But* <u>**those who desire to be rich fall into temptation and a snare**</u>*, and into many foolish and harmful lusts* <u>**which drown men in destruction**</u> *and perdition. For the love of money is a root of all kinds of evil, for which some* have <u>**strayed from the faith in their greediness**</u>*, and pierced themselves through with many sorrows* (1 Tim 6:9-10, NKJV).

It is also important to note that in the parable of the sower Jesus made it plain that **money and the cares of this world** hinder the crop of fruit called faith, which God is looking for in our lives.

> *As for what was sown among thorns, this is he who hears the Word,* <u>**but the cares of the world and the pleasure and delight and glamour and deceitfulness of riches choke and suffocate the Word**</u>*, and it yields* <u>**no fruit**</u> (Matt 13:22, AMP).

More than anything else Jesus is looking for followers who are filled with genuine faith in His word alone when He returns to this earth.

> *When the Son of Man comes, will He really find faith on the earth?"* (Luke 18:8, NKJV)

Chapter 4

Prosperity—Dominionism and World Transformation

Jesus made it plain that **His kingdom** is not of this present world (John 18:36)—and that we were not to become entangled in the **affairs of this life**. Therefore, there is no way to establish the kingdom of God *on earth right now*—without becoming entangled in the affairs of this life on earth.

> *And as Christ's soldier,* <u>do not let yourself become tied up in the affairs of this life</u> (world), *for then you cannot satisfy the one who has enlisted you in his army* (2 Tim 2:4, NLT, parenthesis mine).

Kingdom Now—World Transformation

Howbeit, the *"prosperity doctrine"* and another false doctrine known as the *"societal transformation"* doctrine have merged together with the ambitious agenda of <u>establishing the kingdom right now on earth</u>. Leaders of the "World Transformation" movement are teaching the doctrine of the *transference of wealth* (as mentioned in the previous chapter) for the purpose of *"world transformation."* This transference of wealth for world transformation is dependent upon the false prosperity doctrine to legitimize the "desire" for wealth, which as explained in the previous chapter, is forbidden by the Bible. Proponents for these doctrines use the model for prayer that Jesus gave us in (Matt 6:10) as the premise for establishing Christ's kingdom on earth now "**...Thy kingdom** *come, thy will be done*—**on earth** *as it is in heaven."*

It is imperative therefore, to scripturally establish **what** the kingdom of is and **where** the *kingdom of God* is located during this time (before the return of Jesus). The first Scriptural truth that cannot be set aside or overlooked is the fact that the kingdom of God is found WITHIN every true believer.

> *Now when He was asked by the Pharisees when the kingdom of God would come, He answered them and said, "The kingdom of God does not come with observation... nor will they say,'See here!' or 'See there!'* **For indeed, the kingdom of God is within you** *"* (Luke 17:20-21, NKJV).

This text makes it very clear as to WHERE the kingdom is to be found NOW. The kingdom of God is found WITHIN a believer—where it remains UNTIL it is time for Jesus to come back and RESTORE ALL THINGS (Acts 3:21). It is not until Jesus returns to earth that He will set up a literal kingdom. Therefore, in the model prayer of (Matt 6:10) when we are told to ask for God's KINGDOM TO COME—we are being told to ask that God's kingdom be established within *people*. What God wants to establish WITHIN people is also very clearly stated.

> **For the kingdom of God is** *not eating and drinking; but* **righteousness, and peace, and joy in the Holy Spirit** *(Rom 14:17, NKJV).*

God wants His *righteousness—peace—joy* established within humanity through the preaching of the *gospel of the kingdom*. Those preaching the *world transformation* doctrine falsely define **the**

kingdom of God as the establishment of <u>God's rule</u> upon **the earth—** NOW (not when Christ returns). They advocate the establishing of the kingdom of God by <u>demonstrating righteousness</u> which is being falsely defined as *political justice* within every nation and city. They teach this will bring <u>peace</u> which is being falsely defined as *material and financial prosperity* that will ultimately bring <u>joy</u> which means *happiness* and *personal satisfaction* to the populace. There is also a great emphasis being placed upon achieving *unity* through *tolerance*, with tolerance being used as a major key, in unifying cultural, theological and philosophical differences; in order to be able to come together to build this *transformed new world order*.[9] However, unity based upon tolerance only leads to compromise.

This sounds like a very noble and godly agenda, until one understands that these things are not being advocated by God, but much of what is being taught is contrary to God's word and is deceiving many into following *another gospel* which is opening them up to *another spirit* and preaching *another Jesus*. The lust for *power, wealth* and *recognition* has led many to embrace these and other false teachings.

One such proponent of world transformation is Ed Silvoso founder of *Harvest Evangelism*. In a recent article (advertising one of his many conferences)[10] he relayed a testimony that illustrates just how the transformation doctrine is deceiving people into thinking they are *demonstrating the gospel of the kingdom*. He relays the following testimony from a woman who calls herself a *market place* minister.

> *"As a manager, Rosalynd knew that talking about religion is not typically encouraged, but the Lord began opening doors with many of her employees who would come to her seeking counsel about everyday life situations. She responded by giving them* **<u>kingdom-oriented advice</u>** *in a natural language that they understood. Soon, it was as if her whole team shifted into a different*

---

[9] See chapter 7 of the book *IF POSSIBLE Even the Very Elect Will Be Deceived* by Karen Connell
[10] He is charging a $300 deposit to attend this conference in October, 2012 with a total conference package price of $1,675. Is this his way of receiving the *transference of our wealth to him*?

*thinking as **the spiritual climate improved**. She next found herself able to speak to her district manager, other managers, and even the company owners **about God's role in her management** and **what it means to welcome Jesus in**, both **personally** and **corporately**! The change in the spiritual climate was then accompanied by additional blessings in the natural:*

- *Rosalynd's store was more profitable in 2011 than it was in the past 5 years, having surpassed all its financial goals.*
- *She received a bonus every quarter because sales, cost of goods and labor budgets were all to plan, if not better.*
- *The morale of Rosalynd's team is exceptionally high and an unusual percentage of her employees go on to greater positions like assistant manager in other Jamba Juice locations."*

The above account is a classic example of some the *subtle* false teaching that is being promoted by these self-proclaimed apostles of this transformation doctrine. Please notice the phrase in this woman's testimony where she stated that she gave coworkers **kingdom-oriented advice.** This means she has been taught to *covertly* give Biblical principles to unbelievers thinking this is how you fulfill the Great Commission given to the church, which is that of *going into all the world and preaching the gospel of the kingdom.* Teaching people to be *covert minsters* of kingdom principles is being advocated by those teaching the transformation doctrine. Neither Jesus, or the Apostle Paul nor any of the New Testament writers ever taught this. In fact they taught us to be **BOLD** witnesses not **COVERT** witnesses. The Apostle Paul said…

For I live in eager expectation and hope that I will never do anything that causes me shame, **but that I will always be bold for Christ,** *as I have been in the past, and that my life will always honor Christ, whether I live or I die.* (Phil 1:20, NLT).

Ministering *covertly* is NOT how the Bible says we are to share the gospel of the kingdom—as advocated by another transformation teacher, Lance Wallnau, who wrote the following"

> *Jesus says, "Go into the entire world, all its systems, its mind molders and its Nations and infiltrate the world with My power [signs and wonders] and teachings [commandments]. Go through the door of globalization- world economics- and while it is yet day, while opportunity exists, penetrate these nations and systems with **a demonstration** of a **belief system** that has superior power and results. This is what Daniel did in Babylon and what Joseph did in Egypt. This is a large part of the reason why God is blowing on the marketplace message in this hour. This is a day where third world nations are asking for help, and developing nations are seeking to trade. The window is wide open to the church to impact the world. Opportunity is everywhere."* [11]

This man who is preaching the transformation gospel tells us we are to transform organizations and whole nations by **covertly** getting them to follow the teachings of Christ! He goes on to say:

> *"That's right- you can be covert! One friend of mine is transforming entire schools and businesses by applying certain key commandments to his client's lives and systems.* **They are not even aware of the degree to which (they or) their organizations are being aligned with the teachings of Christ**. *All they know is that it's working. In schools the students are getting better grades and discipline problems are on the decline. In business the people are starting to work like real teams and treating each other with respect. Companies are prospering. It works! (Emphasis, parenthesis & underline mine).*

---

[11] Information provided at a seminar by Dr. Lance Wallnau - www.lancelearning.com

Jesus Christ and His gospel is not a belief system or a set of principles that are to be practiced *covertly* so that students can behave better, get better grades, or cause companies to prosper or help people groups to come out of poverty! Jesus did not come to transform society and make the world a nicer or better place in which to live. He came to save sinners so they would not end up in hell for eternity!

> *...Christ Jesus came into the world to save sinners.*
> *(1 Tim 1:15) KJV*

Boldly (not covertly) proclaiming the true gospel will let people know they are sinners and that they need saving from hell's eternal punishment...

> *But I'll tell you whom to fear. Fear God, who has the power to kill people and then throw them into hell. (Luke 12:5) NLT*

Every person is going to face God in judgment. This is not a popular message that will win you a lot of true converts and friends neither will it impress those who are wealthy. Quite the contrary! It will offend many and find only a few who are willing to respond in true repentance, because the true gospel message makes people see the reality of their sin and the majority of people in the world are trying everything and anything to keep from seeing how sinful they really are. Many sinners however, have no problem receiving *covert* ministry, because it requires nothing of them, other than the desire for success in some area, or some form of self-enhancement and who doesn't want this? False ministers are preaching a cheap imitation gospel that offers a wonderful "rewards program" and those preaching this false gospel are not being truthful about the realities of a hell with its unquenchable fire and eternal torment! This repels people and makes them very uncomfortable and resistant to listening to the truth of the true gospel.

> *God did not send his Son into the world to condemn it, but to save it... "There is no judgment awaiting those who trust him. But those who do not trust him have already been judged for not believing in the only Son of God... Their judgment is based on this fact: The light from heaven came into the world, but they loved the darkness more than the light, for their actions*

> *were evil... They hate the light because they want to sin in the darkness. They stay away from the light for fear their sins will be exposed and they will be punished* (John 3:17-20, NLT).

It is for these very reasons that this false transformation doctrine teaches *covert ministry*. However, we as Bible-believing Christians are not doing the true work of our ministry, if we are not preparing people for their day of judgment by preaching the true gospel of repentance from sin and faith in Jesus Christ. Likewise Christian ministers are not doing the work of their ministry if they are not equipping believers to preach and teach this true gospel message. We are not called to win friends and influence people by trying to transform governments, school systems, the media or arts; but we are called to transform people by getting them to agree with truth concerning their sinful condition and their eternal destiny! We are told:

> *To open their eyes so they may turn from darkness to light, and from the power of Satan to God. Then they will receive forgiveness for their sins and be given a place among God's people, who are set apart by faith in me.'* (Acts 26:18) NLT

Going back to the testimony of the woman mentioned in Ed Silvoso's article, she went on to say that she was... *able to speak to her district manager, other managers, and even the company owners* **about God's role in her management** *and* **what it means to welcome Jesus in**, *both personally and corporately!* Who wouldn't welcome Jesus in to their life or company if they were being promised transformation from poverty to prosperity as a blessing from God? Would these people be so open to "welcoming" Jesus into their lives and businesses if they were given the true gospel and told *to count the cost* that is really required for following Him? In fact how many of those who call themselves *apostles* today would be willing to pay the price that our first apostles paid for simply "preaching the true gospel of Jesus Christ?" According to both tradition and church history the first true apostles suffered horribly at the hands of their persecutors. They did not try to wage war against the devil, but instead they endured suffering as a good soldier, and were willing to partake in the fellowship of Christ's sufferings as we too must be willing to do. Did these true apostles of Christ not have enough faith, revelation, authority or power to overcome the enemy? Satan and his demons most assuredly were motivating their tormentors, yet they didn't fight against the demonic powers that were at work. Here is the great price these true saints and apostles of God paid for doing the work of the ministry.

1. **Matthew** ...Suffered martyrdom in Ethiopia, killed by a sword wound.

2. **Mark** ...Died in Alexandria, Egypt, after being dragged by horses through the streets until he was dead.

3. **Luke** ...Was hanged in Greece as a result of his tremendous preaching to the lost.

4. **John** ...Faced martyrdom when he was boiled in huge basin of boiling oil during a wave of persecution in Rome. However, he was miraculously delivered from death. John was then sentenced to the mines on the prison island of Patmos. He wrote his prophetic Book of Revelation on Patmos. The apostle John was later freed and returned to serve as Bishop of Edessa in modern Turkey. He died as an old man, the only apostle to die peacefully.

5. **Peter** ...He was crucified upside down on an x-shaped cross. According to church tradition it was because he told his tormentors that he felt unworthy to die in the same way that Jesus Christ had died.

6. **James** ...the Just The leader of the church in Jerusalem, was thrown over a hundred feet down from the southeast pinnacle of the Temple when he refused to deny his faith in Christ. When they discovered that he survived the fall, his enemies beat James to death with a fuller's club. This was the same pinnacle where Satan had taken Jesus during the Temptation.

7. **James** ...the Great, Son of Zebedee, was a fisherman by trade when Jesus called him to a lifetime of ministry. As a strong leader of the church, James was ultimately beheaded at Jerusalem. The Roman officer who guarded James watched amazed as James defended his faith at his trial. Later, the officer walked beside James to the place of execution. Overcome by conviction, he declared his new faith to the judge and knelt beside James to accept beheading as a Christian.

8. **Bartholomew** Also known as Nathaniel, was a missionary to Asia. He witnessed for our Lord in present day Turkey. Bartholomew was martyred for his preaching in Armenia where he was flayed to death by a whip.

9. **Andrew** …Was crucified on an x-shaped cross in Patras , Greece. After being whipped severely by seven soldiers they tied his body to the cross with cords to prolong his agony. His followers reported that, when he was led toward the cross, Andrew saluted it in thesewords: 'I have long desired and expected this happy hour. The cross has been consecrated by the body of Christ hanging on it.' He continued to preach to his tormentors for two days until he expired.

10. **Thomas** … Was stabbed with a spear in India during one of his missionary trips to establish the church in the sub-continent.

11. **Jude** …Was killed with arrows when he refused to deny his faith in Christ.

12. **Matthias** …The apostle chosen to replace the traitor Judas Iscariot, was stoned and then beheaded.

13. **Paul** …Was tortured and then beheaded by the evil Emperor Nero at Rome in A.D. 67. Paul endured a lengthy imprisonment, which allowed him to write his many epistles to the churches he had formed throughout the Roman Empire. These letters, which taught many of the foundational doctrines of Christianity, form a large portion of the New Testament. Perhaps this is a reminder to us that our sufferings here are indeed minor compared to the intense persecution and cold cruelty faced by the apostles/disciples during their times for the sake of the Faith. "And ye shall be hated of all men for my name's sake:

> ***""But he that endures to the end shall be saved"***
> (Matthew10:22, KJV).

The word *suffering* for the cause of preaching the true gospel is not in the vocabulary of these modern day self-proclaimed apostles. The word suffering has been replaced by the word *overcomer*. We are told we don't have to put up with suffering—meaning we have the authority to OVERCOME anything we don't like. Many have come to believe we just have to declare war upon the enemy and we can alter our circumstances by spiritually warring our way out of our suffering.[12] May we never forget, the term *overcomer* is associated with those who overcame sin (which includes deception) before they die. We will not be clothed in white and declared to be an overcomer if we defile ourselves by believing and preaching doctrines of demons! Jesus said that those...

> *... Who have not defiled their garments... they shall walk with Me in white, for they are worthy...* **He who overcomes shall be clothed in white garments**, *and I will not blot out his name from the Book of Life; but I will confess his name before My Father and before His angels.* (Rev 3:4-5, NKJV)

We must be willing to participate in and endure the fellowship of Christ's sufferings, whether it be through receiving the rejection and mocking scorn of sinners when we try to convince them of their sin and their need for Christ as their Savior—or suffering that comes because of our acts of obedience to God's word which result in the **loss** of *popularity, power* or *privileges* because of not following the world ways of doing things. Then there is also a suffering that God Himself ordains as a means to purify us from defilement—yes God will bring suffering into our lives for the purpose of purifying us, just as Job found out!

> *Yet indeed I also count all things loss...that I may know Him and the power of His resurrection, and the fellowship of His sufferings, being conformed to His death...* (Phil 3:8, 10, NKJV).

The Authority of the Believe

Another false teaching spawned by the word of faith movement and carried on into the world transformation movement is called **THE AUTHORITY OF THE BELIEVER.** This teaching says we can be just like Jesus—having all the authority, power and wisdom of Jesus

---

[12] This kind of thinking comes from the false *faith and patience* mentioned on pages 23 & 25.

right now, because as Saints of God we are created in God's image. Bill Hamon, a transformation advocate stated the following;

> *Adam and Eve failed. So Jesus came 4,000 years later to reactivate the plan of God. He recreated a human race as we were recreated in Christ Jesus. We are a new creation, born again, children of God. This new creation's purpose is to be conformed into the image of Jesus Christ.* **That's just not in holiness and purity, but to be like Jesus in every way of His authority, power, wisdom, grace**, *the way He thinks, the way He acts, to have His government and His principles. We are supposed to be a* **full personification** *and manifestation and demonstration* **of who Christ is** *and what Christ is like. And Christ is a full demonstration of who God is and what God is like.*[13]

The premise for the above statement by Bill Hamon, is that all Saints can **demonstrate all the authority, power, wisdom, and grace of Jesus NOW—because we are just like Jesus is now.** The only way we could possibly be just like Jesus now is if we were now living in our **glorified body**! Those with glorified bodies will no longer be subject to the temptations of their flesh (fallen nature). This of course will not happen until we meet Jesus in the air when we are taken off this earth to receive our glorified body and become perfected. Until then we do not have the ***full personification*** of Christ as God!

> ***For we*** (now) ***know in part, and we prophesy in part... But*** ***when that which is perfect is come*** (our perfection or glorification) ***then that which is in part shall be done away*** (1 Cor 13:9-10, KJV).

Until our perfection or glorification comes, all true believers need God's *spiritual gifts* to operate, and even with these our power is only in *in part*. This means we only have as much of God's power as

---

[13] http://www.thevoicemagazine.com/ApoMoments_BillHamon.htm (emphasis mine)

demonstrated through God's spiritual gifts as the Holy decides to give to each of us. He alone decides what gifts we will be given. The above statement by Bill Hamon makes it sound like we are equal to God in every way through authority, power, wisdom and grace! This again is Satan's egotistical desire...*to be like the most High!* There is coming a time when we shall become *like Him,* but this does not happen until Christ returns for us—then we shall be transformed into His glorified image.

> *Yes, dear friends, we are already God's children, and <u>we can't even imagine what we</u> <u>WILL BE LIKE when Christ returns</u>. But we do know that <u>when he comes we will be like</u> <u>him</u>, (receive our glorified bodies) for we will see him as he really is... And all who believe this <u>will keep themselves pure</u>, just as Christ is pure* (1 John 3:2-3, NLT).

The Christ-like image we are to be conformed to NOW is the one that Jesus modeled for us while He lived on earth before His death and resurrection (before He was glorified). He was a human who had the Holy Spirit of God living within Him—just as all true believers have. He was able to operate in the gifts of the Holy Spirit through the power of the Holy Spirit that lived within Him—just as any true believer can. He modeled a life of godly character and wisdom to overcome sin and Satan, through the authority of God's word—just as any true believer must. However, he did nothing on His own, even though He was the Son of God. Everything He did was according to His faith—that came as a result of hearing from God His Father first, just as we must do.

> *For I have not spoken on <u>My own authority</u>; but the Father who sent Me gave Me a command...* (John 12:49, NKJV).

As Believers we too are sons (children of God) but like Jesus we too must learn humility by depending on God and His word for our authority. This means we do not have ALL AUTHORITY over our circumstances or the current state of affairs in this sin sick world. We cannot ago about making *authoritative declarations* because we desire to see positive changes in negative circumstances. The only authority we as believers have comes through *rightly dividing* the word of God by hearing the Holy Spirit teach us what we need to hear.

There is coming a time when God's people shall rule with Jesus upon the earth and subdue the nations—but now is not that time. Trying to establish God's kingdom on this earth before it's time is not the work of the Holy Spirit but the prideful presumptuous work of another spirit called the anti-christ spirit of Satan.

> *He* (anti-christ) ***shall speak <u>pompous words</u> against*** (contrary to) ***the Most High, Shall persecute the saints of the Most High, <u>And shall intend to change times and law</u>. Then the saints shall be given into his hand For a time and times and half a time*** (Dan 7:25, NKJV, parenthesis mine).

My husband and I were part of Bill Hamon's ministerial association for a number of years, and we were finally forced to leave his association when we began to see the error that was very *subtly* being taught.

A big part of his ministry is that of holding training sessions where Christians are given the opportunity to be *activated* in the *spiritual gifts*. These activations are preceded by a series of teachings on the spiritual gifts which use and misuse Scriptures to convince those desiring to be activated in the gifts, of false ideas concerning how one can operate and manifest spiritual gifts.[14] The emphasis in operating in spiritual gifts is the foundation for Bill Hamon's ministry because he believes it is the avenue for what he says is a *"<u>full personification</u> ... <u>of God Himself</u>!*" He even goes so far as to say that holiness is not a factor when it comes to operating in spiritual gifts. We just need to believe that God wants us to operate in the gifts, and not let the issue of holiness get in the way of having faith for receiving spiritual gifts!

This desperation for Christians to operate in *supernatural power*

---

[14] Having gone through the Spiritual Gifts training at C.I.— We found that much Scripture is used to enforce a number of Bill Hamon's ideas regarding the operation of gifts, however these Scriptures were often misused and even contradicted other Scriptures on the same subject.

(spiritual gifts—signs and wonders) is because without these we cannot *demonstrate the kingdom of God* (which is another false teaching I will address shortly). Leaders like Bill Hamon are placing great emphasis upon Christians being able to operate in the supernatural anytime they see the need. Bill Hamon teaches such things as we can prophesy anytime we desire—just as we can speak in tongues anytime we desire. Therefore—we can demonstrate supernatural signs and wonders *anytime we desire*.

Again, when I hear this kind of teaching I can only think of what Lucifer said before being expelled from heaven...***I will be like the most High*** (Isa 14:14, KJV). Being created in God's image does not make us "like the most High" in power and authority—this again is what Satan desired. They also teach that any of the nine gifts of the Holy Spirit can be **imparted** to others by those who have these gifts.

What is not emphasized by this false *impartation* teaching—concerning spiritual gifts, is the fact that it is only the HOLY SPIRIT, not those who have His gifts—who decides who will be given what gifts by God and when they will be operated in. They are His gifts to be used when He desires them to be used. We can lay hands on other believers and ask the Holy Spirit to impart whatever gift **He decides to give them**, but we have no authority or power to impart gifts to those who desire them.[15]

> *It is the one and only Holy Spirit who distributes these gifts. He alone decides which gift each person should have* (1 Cor 12:11, NLT).

Yes, we are to desire the gifts, but it is still up to the Holy Spirit to decides to whom and when they should be given and WHEN they should be used. This is why I emphasize over and over that *true faith* comes ONLY by HEARING God speak to us (Rom 10:17). Unless we *hear the Holy Spirit tell us* to use a certain gift at a particular time...we are acting out of presumption and are not being led by Him, but are in danger of being led by our flesh or by another spirit that we may be "hearing" from. The only way we as believers can *impart our gifts* to

---

[15] For an in depth study on the subject of "spiritual gifts", see author's *Spiritual Gifts Manual* at www.extendedlife.net

anyone is by faith using our gifts (when directed by the Holy Spirit) for the purpose of *establishing* others in true faith.

> *For I long to see you, that I may impart to you some spiritual gift, so that you may be established — that is, that I may be encouraged together with you by the mutual faith both of you and me* (Rom 1:11-12, NKJV).

Demonstrating the Kingdom of God

A Demonstration of POWER, through signs and wonders, is how NAR (New Apostolic Reformation) leaders are teaching we are to *demonstrate the kingdom of God.* Therefore the establishment of the *kingdom of God* is being defined by world transformation advocates as anyplace signs and wonders are being used to transform or change for the better people's circumstances. They heavily advertise for people to come to their conferences to receive a spiritual impartation (which of course requires one to pay fair amount of money to attend) in order to receive the power to do "miracles" so we can demonstrate and establish the kingdom of God. In an article from his website Bill Hamon says: [16]

> *"Knowing Christ Jesus only as Saviour, Healer, Baptizer, Provider, etc.* **is no longer sufficient!** *We must now know Him also as King of kings, Lord of our lives and the Commander of the Lord's army...we can take* **the gospel of the Kingdom to a world that needs a demonstration of the lordship of Christ.** *The gifts of the Spirit are not toys for the saints to play with in church. They are mighty weapons of war! God has provided them* **so we can take** *territories and nations..."* (Emphasis mine).

---

[16]This article can be read in its entirety at:
https://www.christianinternational.com/index.php?option=com_zoo&task=item&item_id=2742&Itemid=68

If you are not aware of how certain well known phrases such as *the gospel of Kingdom* and the *demonstration of the lordship of Christ* are being re-defined…you probably would not have a problem with the above statement. For instance, Christians are being told that demonstrating supernatural powers is how a Christian <u>demonstrates the lordship of Christ</u> and it is also how we <u>demonstrate the gospel of the kingdom</u>. Demonstrating the lordship of Christ is not about demonstrating spiritual gifts or supernatural signs and wonders. The lordship of Christ is however, about living a life of Christ-like character (holiness—humility) and obedience to God and His Word. This is what Jesus said about His lordship:

> **"So why do you call me 'Lord,' when you won't obey me?** (Luke 6:46, NLT).

The way we *demonstrate* the *lordship* of Jesus to others then, is not through supernatural power, but through obeying the word of God (not contradicting it)! Lordship is demonstrated through living a holy and pure life that honors Jesus Christ and brings glory to God. There is a time and place for signs and wonders but these are not how we demonstrate the lordship of Jesus to a world that does not know Him. Also the *gospel of the kingdom* is to PREACHED not *demonstrated* by supernatural signs and wonders. In order for the gospel to be effective, people must see their sin and their need for the Savior. Bringing the message of repentance from sin and the GOOD NEWS of forgiveness through faith in Christ must be PROMCLAIMED boldly. Signs and wonders did not lead people to repentance it only fed their greedy hearts. We read in (Jn 12:37)…

> **But although He had done so many signs before them, they did not believe in Him.**

Those who can demonstrate *supernatural power* or the ability to create *wealth* are highly recognized by the leaders of the NAR (New Apostolic Reformation) movement, of which Bill Hamon is a key leader. In fact one such preacher that was highly acclaimed and fully embraced by NAR leaders was Todd Bentley. We had already pulled out of Bill Hamon's organization before Bentley became known for his *signs and wonders* meetings in Lakeland, Florida during 2008. It was also during this time that I was directed by the Lord to write my book on deception. [17] During the time of Todd Bentley's meetings we were still on CI's mailing list and received a CD with a personal message from Bill Hamon fully endorsing Todd Bentley's ministry and the signs and wonders he was operating in. It was shortly after this that C. Peter Wagner and many other minsters associated with the NAR publicly proclaimed Todd Bentley to be an apostle. Anyone with any discernment at all should have seen this man as a false minster who was operating in lying signs and wonders! Of course not longer after he was publically embraced by the NAR, he was found to be in adultery and eventually divorced his wife in order to marry the woman he had an affair with.

This should give many involved with this "new move" known as the New Apostolic Reformation (NAR), reason to start looking more closely at its leaders and what they teach. Perversion of God's word and sexual perversion go hand in hand. A study of our modern day fallen church leaders bears this out.

Those who are advocating world transformation and teaching that we are to DEMONSTRATE the kingdom of God by doing supernatural signs and wonders—misuse what Paul said in (1 Cor 4:20) ***...For the kingdom of God is not in word but in power***. A closer examination of this verse reveals it is being taken out of context to promote a false premise. Paul said in the *context of this verse* that he would not be swayed by what was spoken by those who were proud, but he was looking for the *dunamis*—supernatural "can do" power or ability to become Christ-like in their character (holy and humble), which is sorely lacking among the leaders of this NAR movement and among many of its followers.

> ***...as my beloved children I warn you... For though you might have ten thousand instructors in Christ, yet you do not have many fathers; for in Christ Jesus I have begotten you through the gospel*** (of repentance and salvation)**...** ***Therefore I urge you, imitate me*** (in Christ-like holy and humble character)**...** ***For this reason I have sent***

---

[17] Karen Connell, *EVEN THE VERY ELECT Will Be Deceived*, published by Lulu Publishing Co.

> *Timothy to you, who is my beloved and faithful son in the Lord, who will remind you <u>of my ways in Christ</u>,* (manner of life) *as I teach everywhere in every church... Now some are puffed up, as though I were not coming to you... But I will come to you shortly, if the Lord wills, and <u>I will know, not the word of those who are puffed up</u>,* but the power... *For the kingdom of God is not in word but in power* (1 Cor 4:14-20, NKJV, parenthesis mine).

This verse has nothing whatsoever to do with **demonstrating signs and wonders** to establish the literal kingdom of God upon the earth. Paul was talking about having the power to demonstrate a life that was *righteous-peaceful-joyous* with *Christ-like character*, which is only possible through God's indwelling supernatural *dunamis* power. That is why he said he was looking for a *demonstration of power*. In other words the Apostle Paul was saying "actions speak louder than words" when it comes to calling yourself a Christian. We must demonstrate Christ-likeness in our character (not in our ability to do supernatural works).

It is no wonder there is such an emphasis on doing *supernatural signs and wonders* by those teaching false doctrines. Satan knows that supernatural signs and wonders, will deceive those who are *ignorant* or choose to ignore God's word and those who are *greedy*. Many are being taught and deceived into thinking that by following Christ they can obtain POWER, WEALTH and AUTHORITY that can transform the lives, cities and nations of the world causing them to be *recognized* as *super-saints*. It all comes back to Satan's same old agenda—seeking *power—wealth—recognition* (worship). It is very appealing to those in pride to think they are able to see relationships, homes, jobs, cities or nations changed for the better because of believing they have been given *all power* to become *like God* and transform these things?

False ministers also know that if their followers pursue "prosperity and wealth" they can collect more "seed" through their conferences, books, CD's—DVD's, video conferences, cruises and a host of other *merchandising schemes* that promote these false teachings—which in turn enlarges their treasuries. As the saying goes "just follow the money" and you will find the false motivation for why people are doing what they do. May we never forget that one of the reasons Satan was cast out of heaven was because of his lust for "merchandising" which was all part of his agenda to build and establish a kingdom of his own. This same *kingdom establishing mentality* is also promoted through the NAR (New Apostolic Reformation) movement!

> **By the multitude of your merchandise** *they have filled the midst of you with violence* (injustice), *and you have sinned* (Ezek 28:16, NKJV).

The Seven Mountains False Doctrine

Christians worldwide are now being told to take dominion over and control *seven mind-molding "kingdoms"* of this world known as the **"seven mountains"** found in every nation on earth. These "seven mountains" are said to be...

- **Family**
- **Education**
- **Media**
- **Arts-entertainment**
- **Business-medical**
- religion
- government-politics

The NAR (New Apostolic Reformation) says that WE ARE to *take back* these "kingdoms" of the world and make them subject to the rule of Christ. This sounds GOOD, but in reality this is the EVIL genius of Satan himself. The problem lies in the fact that these false teachers are again taking Scripture out of context to convince unwary Christians to become steeped in the cares and affairs of this life and deceived into thinking this is how they are to establish the kingdom of God on earth and transform nations. A big emphasis in this move includes a multitude of merchandising schemes—steeped in "false prosperity" teachings. Those who do not "rightly divide" the word of truth are being deceived into thinking that we are to establish the kingdom of God upon the earth through these "seven mountains" —

We must not be fooled by those preaching doctrines of demons. One such proponent of this new move even promotes *covertly* applying

"God's commandments" in order to bring about positive changes in these "seven mountains." Nowhere are we told to "covertly" establish the kingdom of God—we are told to boldly preach the true gospel of the kingdom (repentance and forgiveness through faith in Jesus Christ).

This positive change sounds GOOD but it is EVIL—because it is a work of man and not a work of God. It is interesting to me that the only time the term "seven mountains" is mentioned in the Bible is when they are seen on the head of the Satanic beast upon which the spirit of harlotry (idolatry) rides.

> *I saw a woman sitting on a scarlet beast... having* **seven heads....** *"Here is the mind which has wisdom:* **The seven heads are seven mountains** *on which the woman sits.* (Rev 17:3, 9 NKJV).

The leaders in the NAR movement also teach that Jesus can't come back until ALL THINGS ARE RESTORED (by us—the saints of God) and until then Jesus must remain in heaven. Again they misuse the Scripture in (Acts 3:21) as a basis for this:

> ***For he must remain in heaven*** **until the time** *for the final restoration of all things, as God promised* **long ago** *through his prophets.* NLT

They claim that the "time" for "all things" to be restored is **now**, and it is to be done by the Church which has now been **fully restored**. However, this and many other portions of Scripture are clear that when it is **TIME** for all things to be restored—it will be when Jesus comes back to earth with us His **glorified** saints. This will happen just as the Old Testament prophets described. Therefore, we are not in that **TIME** when we should be trying to restore all things.

The Scriptures being used to support these false teachings are again being taken out context to support these false ideas. For one thing the Church has not been fully restored as they teach—so we the Church cannot "transform" anything, because we have not yet been transformed into His image! A close look around our churches makes this very plain to see. The church will not become glorious until it has been glorified...

> *...the glorious church without spot, wrinkle or any such blemish* (Eph 5:27)

It isn't UNTIL we are **perfected** (brought to completion by being glorified) that we will become the "glorious" (unified and glorified) church. As it stands now there are many divisions and false doctrines among us, because we do not yet *see Christ as He really is* (1 Jn 3:2). We have not come to a *complete* (perfected) *knowledge of Jesus* (the word) so there is not yet the unity that the glorified body will have. The text in (Eph 4:11-24) is being miss-taught because certain verses are being pulled out their context to support a false premise in many cases. This text is actually telling us that...

> *(vs. 11-12) And He Himself gave some to be apostles, some prophets, some evangelists, and some pastors and teachers... for the equipping of* <u>**the saints**</u> *for* <u>**the work of ministry**</u>*, for the* <u>**edifying**</u> *of the body of Christ,*
>
> *(vs. 13)* <u>**UNTIL**</u> (we reach the point where [18]) *we ALL come to the* <u>**unity of the faith**</u> *and of the* <u>**knowledge of the Son of God**</u>*, to* (BECOME) *a* <u>**perfect man**</u> (a perfected glorified body of true saints)*, to the measure of the stature* <u>**of the fullness of Christ**</u>*;*

It isn't UNTIL we reach the point where the 5-fold ministry is no longer needed to equip the saints for their ministry of reigning with Christ that this time of preparation and equipping ends. At what point does this equipping by the 5-fold ministers end? It is when we (the true church) become a *perfect man* (glorified) and finally come to the place of reaching *the fullness of Christ* (to be fully like Him). Then we will have *the unity of faith* (all true Christians believing the same thing)

---

[18] The word *until* (Strong's #3360) **mechri** (mekh'-ree) refers to a time up to a certain point and implying that the action terminates there. Thus the equipping of the saints for the work of the ministry by the 5-fold ministry in (vs. 11-12) ends when (vs. 13) happens. The Complete Word Study Dictionary: New Testament © 1992 by AMG

because we as glorified saints will all see Him as He is and finally have the perfected *knowledge of the Son of God!*

Until we reach this point of becoming the perfect man (the glorified church) we are told ...

> *...that we should no longer be children, tossed to and fro and carried about with every wind of doctrine, by the trickery of men, in the cunning craftiness of deceitful plotting... but, speaking the truth in love, may grow up in all things into Him who is the head Christ... from whom the whole body, joined and knit together by what every joint supplies, according to the effective working by which every part does its share, causes growth of the body for the edifying of itself in love... This I say, therefore, and testify in the Lord, that you should no longer walk as the rest of the Gentiles walk, in the futility of their mind.. having their understanding darkened, being alienated from the life of God, because of the ignorance that is in them, because of the blindness of their heart...who, being past feeling, have given themselves over to lewdness, to work all uncleanness with greediness...But you have not so learned Christ...* <u>**if indeed you have heard Him and have been taught by Him, as the truth is in Jesus**</u>*...that you put off, concerning your former conduct, the old man which grows corrupt according to the deceitful lusts... and be renewed in the spirit of your mind...and that you put on the new man which was created according to God, in true righteousness and holiness (Eph 4:11-24 NKJV).*

The above text simply put is telling us *two* things we should be doing UNTIL we become glorified saints. The first thing is—we should concentrate on HEARING from Jesus (vs. 21) because true faith comes by hearing, then we don't embrace false doctrines. Secondly, we should concentrate on keeping darkness from invading our minds so we can live holy sanctified lives for God.

When Jesus comes back and we are glorified we the *resurrected saints* will then help Jesus put down all His enemies during His millennial reign. Then nations will be transformed by the glory of God, and not by the glory of man. *And they* (the resurrected saints) ***lived and reigned with Christ for a thousand years*** (Rev 20:4, NKJV) Jesus (not us) establishes His Kingdom on earth—**after** He returns to earth—and not before.

> "***..those*** **in Christ all shall be made alive.** *But each one in his own order: Christ the firstfruits, afterward <u>those who are Christ's at</u>* **His coming… Then comes the end,** *when* **He delivers the kingdom** (which is within the true church) **to God the Father,** (this is) *when He puts an end to all rule and all authority and power* (which is contrary to God)*… For He must reign* **(for 1000 years)** *till He has put all enemies under His feet* (1 Cor 15:22-25, NKJV, parenthesis mine).

In my book ***Investigating and Experiencing the Glory of God***, I write the following:

> *"It is important to understand that how we live our life now while on earth is going to determine our eternal destiny and position in God's eternal kingdom, which Jesus (not us) will establish upon this earth. God has a role for those in His millennial kingdom and eternal rule, who are willing to seek Him and know Him intimately **now** while on this earthly journey. The saints of God will be vessels of His glory carrying that glory from the throne of God in heaven to the nations of the earth; for which task we will need glorified bodies. However if we are not sanctified (dedicated) temples filled with His glory that bring glory to God (making God very apparent to others) while here on earth; we will not receive a glorified body and be numbered as one of God's saints—a faithful child of God who is a*

"son brought to glory" (Heb 2:10-11) by the sanctifying fire of God in their life." [19]

It is essential to understand that WE (true believers and followers of Christ) ARE THE KINGDOM (a holy nation) that is presented to God the father at Christ's second coming—because the kingdom is WITHIN us. Therefore, His kingdom must be first established **in us** so His glory can cover the earth **through us** when He returns.

> *Now when He was asked by the Pharisees* **when the kingdom of God would come,** *He answered them and said,* **"The kingdom of God does not come with observation...** *nor will they say, 'See here!' or 'See there!'* **For indeed, the kingdom of God is within you"** (Luke 17:20-21, NKJV).

Establishing the kingdom of God is not about establishing Christian principles within a government, the entertainment industry or improving family relationships, or trying to eradicate poverty in a city or nation, so its people have enough to eat and drink!

> **For the kingdom of God is not eating and drinking,** *but* **righteousness** *and peace and joy in the Holy Spirit* (Rom 14:17,NKJV).

Establishing the kingdom of God is about *transforming* the *spiritual condition* of people and translating them out of their worldly pagan cultures into the spiritual kingdom of God.

> *Who has delivered us from the power of darkness, and has translated us into the kingdom of his dear Son* (Col 1:13, KJV).

The kingdom of God is about getting people right with God through preaching that establishes righteousness through repentance and forgiveness of sin by faith in Christ—then and only then can people have true peace and joy no matter what the conditions are upon the earth! When people get right with God they will no longer be *of*

---

[19] See author's book *Investigating and Experiencing the Glory of God* P. 58

this world or be involved in its "Babylonian"—anti-Christ systems (the "7" mountains)—they will come out from among them as we are told to do!

> *Do not be unequally yoked together with unbelievers. For what fellowship has righteousness with lawlessness? And what communion has light with darkness? ...And what accord has Christ with Belial? Or what part has a believer with an unbeliever? ...And what agreement has the temple of God with idols? For you are the temples of the living God. As God has said: "I will dwell in them And walk among them. I will be their God, And they shall be My people." ...Therefore "<u>Come out from among them And be separate</u>, says the Lord. Do not touch what is unclean, And I will receive you." ...'I will be a Father to you, And you shall be My sons and daughters, Says the LORD Almighty"* (2 Cor 6:17 NKJV).

Our fight is not against the injustice in this world, our fight is the fight of faith—that is founded upon God's word.

> *Jesus answered, "<u>My kingdom is not of this world</u>. If My kingdom were of this world, My servants <u>would fight</u>, so that I should not be delivered to the Jews;* (they were not to fight against the injustice Jesus faced from the Jews) *but now My kingdom is not from here"* (John 18:36, NKJV).

God's kingdom can't be released unless we preach righteousness (the right thing—truth). The truth of the matter is things are going to get much worse and not better. God's chosen people are going to be hated and hunted down, because they choose not to align themselves with the kingdoms of this world. Those willing to compromise for the sake of receiving POWER—WEALTH—RECOGNITION will be willing to get involved in the kingdoms of this world. Therein lays their deception.

However, there is coming a time when *the kingdoms of this*

world will become the kingdoms of our God (Rev 11:15). Until then we must not allow the spirit of anti-christ that is operating through false teachers, prophets and apostles to deceive us by—by *changing the times* as described by the Prophet Daniel (Dan 7:25). This is now being done by misusing Scriptures that refer to the millennial kingdom (which is established on earth by Jesus and His saints when He returns) to teach us we should be establishing the millennial kingdom now. The time for the restoration of all things is at hand—because the return of Christ is at hand. But we are not in the time to restore all things now, as we have already examined. We must not let false teachers tell us our *eschatological beliefs* don't matter, because in the end we all end up in the NEW EARTH. Those who become deceived and defile their garments through deception and false teaching, will not end up on the new earth, but in outer darkness or in the Lake of fire if their deception and sins are not repented of!

> **But the sons of the kingdom** *will be cast out into outer darkness. There will be weeping and gnashing of teeth"* (Matt 8:12, NKJV).
>
> *Blessed are those who do His commandments, that they may have the right to the tree of life, and may enter through the gates into the city…* **But outside are dogs and sorcerers and sexually immoral and murderers and idolaters, and whoever loves and practices a lie** (Rev 22:14-15, NKJV).
>
> *He who overcomes shall inherit all things, and I will be his God and he shall be My son… But the cowardly, unbelieving, abominable, murderers, sexually immoral, sorcerers, idolaters, and all liars shall have their part in the lake which burns with fire and brimstone, which is the second death."*

Our eschatological beliefs do matter, because any error breeds deception that can lead God's people away from the true gospel—the true Jesus and the God's Holy Spirit. Many are already becoming confused and discouraged because they are not seeing all the great things that many false teachers have been promising them. Multitudes of deceived people in the church are laboring and spending vast amounts of resources and time to bring about the changes that false teachers and leaders are advocating for world transformation. We must simply follow the great commission given to us by Jesus— that of trying to reach the lost in every nation with the true gospel of the kingdom, which is repentance from sin and salvation through faith in Christ alone. The will of the Lord for His people is not complicated... it is a very simple.

> *See then that you walk circumspectly, not as fools but as wise... redeeming the time, because the days are evil... Therefore do not be unwise, but understand what the will of the Lord is.* (Eph 5:15-17)

> *But we urge you, brethren, ... that you also aspire to lead a quiet life, to mind your own business, and to work with your own hands, as we commanded you... that you may walk properly toward those who are outside, and that you may lack nothing.* (1 Thess 4:10-12) NKJV

Most of all may we remember this warning: concerning the workings of the anti-christ spirit which is already at work in the world and even with the church...

> *Even if they (false teachers) claim to have had a vision, a revelation... don't believe them...Don't be fooled by what they say. For ... the man of lawlessness (the anti-christ spirit within a person) is revealed — (as) the one who brings destruction. He will position himself in the temple of God, claiming that he himself is God* (2 Tess 2:2-4, NLT).

The truth of the matter is—Jesus is not interested in transforming this present world, and making it into a better place to live before He returns—because He is going to destroy it by fire and start all over again with a **new heavens** and a **new earth!** (2 Pet 3:10-11, 13; Rev 21:1). Why then would we work so hard to transform what is yet to be destroyed by God? Warning people of their sin and bringing them to the knowledge of Christ and on to maturity as Christian disciples is the **only mission** of the church on earth now. We are here to make disciples for Jesus Christ in every nation and in every culture. Getting them ready to become perfected glorified saints of God!

> **...preaching (Christ), warning** *every man and* **teaching** *every man in all wisdom, that we may present every man* **perfect** *in Christ Jesus* (Col 1:28, KJV).

There is only ONE MOUNTAIN that we need to be concerned with and it is called God's Holy Mountain.

> *For on* **My holy mountain,** *on the mountain height of Israel," says the Lord GOD, "there all the house of Israel... shall serve Me* (Ezek 20:40, NKJV).

Mountains in Scripture represent something that is being "promoted." God calls ISRAEL—His chosen people who are known as His "Holy Nation"—His Holy Mountain. God's true saints are to be promoting and making known His righteousness and holiness in every nation. The only way that the nations of the world are going to come to know the one true God, is by true Christians demonstrating who God is *through Christ dwelling in them.* People need to see Christ in us, so they can come to know the Lord our God, rather than seeing a display of supernatural signs and wonders demonstrated on Satan's "7" mountains.

> *"So* **you shall know that I am the LORD your God, Dwelling in Zion** *My holy mountain* (Joel 3:17, NKJV).

There are those dwelling in God's Holy Mountain (His holy nation-the church) who are not willing to receive correction and turn from what is false and evil. There are those leaders who have an image to uphold which they themselves have created. Those in deception, and who are not willing to receive correction, are in pride and will become rebellious against the truth of God's word when it goes against their false ideas or personal agendas. God tells us He is going to do some house cleaning and remove them from His Holy Mountain. ...

> **I will remove all the proud** *and arrogant people from among you.* **There will be no pride on my holy mountain** (Zeph 3:11, NLT).

Pride and rebellion (bitterness) are to have no place in God's people. For only those who love the truth will be part of the Bride of Christ, also known as the city the New Jerusalem that will be...

>...*coming down out of heaven from God, prepared as a bride* adorned *for her husband* (Rev 21:2).

Jesus is coming back for a Bride that will be "adorned" with righteousness and clothed with the truth of God's word. The true Bride of Christ will not have those among who embrace false teaching or false ministers. *"Thus says the LORD:*

> **'I will return to Zion**, *And dwell in the midst of Jerusalem.* **Jerusalem shall be called the City of Truth,** *The Mountain of the LORD of hosts, The Holy Mountain'* (Zech 8:3, NKJV).

But this very simple message and mission are being set aside by those teaching a false *world transformation gospel* by which many who were once true to Christ—are now deceived and defiled.

> *For I am jealous for you with godly jealousy. For I have betrothed you to one husband that I may* **present you as a chaste virgin to Christ**... *But I fear, lest somehow, as the serpent deceived Eve by his craftiness,* **so your minds may be corrupted from the simplicity that is in Christ**.... *For if he who comes preaches* **another Jesus** *whom we have not preached, or if you receive* **a different spirit** *which you have not received, or* **a different gospel** *which you have not accepted — you may well put up with it!* (2 Cor 11:2-4, NKJV).

Satan is out to steal our inheritance (eternal life) found in Christ's kingdom, which is awaiting God's *true saints*. Saints are dedicated to the truth and purity of God's word and Satan is out to defile God's people through deception from false teaching such as Eve received. What Satan told her caused her to and end up calling what God said was evil—good and calling what He said was good—to be seen as evil. We must be true seekers of God and His word and be careful not to fall into following those who preach ANYTHING that is contrary to the Word of God.

> *"...untaught and unstable people twist* (the Scriptures) *to their own destruction ... You therefore, beloved... beware lest you also fall from your own steadfastness,* <u>*being led away with the error of the wicked*</u>*... but grow in the grace and knowledge of our Lord and Savior Jesus Christ. To Him be the glory both now and forever. Amen!* (2 Peter 3:16-18, NKJV).

Conclusion

The Bible is clear then about the kind of *spiritual warfare* that all true believers must be engaged in; which is the battle of contending for the truth of God's word and the true faith. Our fight is against all lies and doubts that the demonic forces of Satan use to create false doctrines that lead God's people away from the true faith, some of which this study has examined. It is imperative that we measure everything we hear taught—by God's Word. There are those who continue to blindly swallow all that they hear coming out of the mouths of their favorite ministers, because it *sounds exciting and even Biblical* but in truth it is not—they are causing their faith to become shipwrecked on the shores of deception.

> *...fight well in the Lord's battles... Cling tightly to your faith in Christ, and always keep your conscience clear. For some people have deliberately violated their consciences; as a result, their faith has been shipwrecked* (1 Tim 1:18-1,9 NLT).

There is a tidal wave of false teaching that has come against the body of Christ and unless we spend time examining ALL that we hear in light of the Scriptures, we will fall prey to these doctrines of demons! If Christ is really dwelling in us we will hear His voice (within our conscience i.e. spirit) tell us that what we are hearing is not according to the truth of God's Word. This voice has many times spared me from embracing that which is false.

> *Hold on to the pattern of right teaching you learned from me. And remember to live in the faith and love*

> *that you have in Christ Jesus…With the help of the Holy Spirit who lives within us, carefully guard what has been entrusted to you* (2 Tim 1:13-14, NLT).

Far too many "Christian" teachers and preachers are using "right words" (Scriptural terms) but are giving them "wrong" meanings. Therefore, the undiscerning embrace what is being taught because they hear *familiar Biblical language* and terms being thrown around, but fail to see that they are being given unscriptural *meanings.* For instance we are told we need to be *militant warriors.* Some, as we have discussed, have taken this to mean we must wage war against the devil and his hierarchy, using all kinds of unscriptural practices, when in reality our battle is a battle for the *true faith.* To be militant is to be vigorously active and aggressive, especially in support of a cause. Many false gospels promote the taking up of many *causes,* such as a fight against injustice, poverty, immoral practices in the government, the arts and entertainment industry, and many more such "noble" sounding causes. We must contend for the truth of God's word in order to keep the true faith. The only *cause* however, that we are to actively, vigorously and aggressively pursue is the "cause of Christ"

> *…our Savior Jesus Christ, who has abolished death and brought life and immortality to light through the gospel…to which I was appointed a preacher, an apostle, and a teacher… For this reason I also suffer these things; nevertheless I am not ashamed, for I know whom I have believed* (2 Tim 1:10-12, NKJV).

As good soldiers of Jesus Christ we must be willing to suffer whatever misunderstanding, rejection and persecution that come our way because of going against the current popular tide of deception and false teachings. We must boldly open our mouths and contend for the truth and true faith found only in Christ.

We have a glorious future to look forward to, we cannot even imagine all that God has prepared for those that love Him and are willing to stay true to His Holy word. Surely the pure in heart will see God and all He has waiting for those who remain faithful to Him.

> *All honor to the God and Father of our Lord Jesus Christ, for it is by his boundless mercy*

that God has given us the privilege of being born again. Now we live with a wonderful expectation because Jesus Christ rose again from the dead... For God has reserved a priceless inheritance for his children. It is kept in heaven for you, pure and undefiled, beyond the reach of change and decay... And God, in his mighty power, will protect you until you receive this salvation, because you are trusting in him. It will be revealed on the last day for all to see....So be truly glad! There is wonderful joy ahead, even though it is necessary for you to endure many trials for a while... These trials are only to test your faith, to show that it is strong and pure. It is being tested as fire tests and purifies gold — and your faith is far more precious to God than mere gold. So if your faith remains strong after being tried by fiery trials, it will bring you much praise and glory and honor on the day when Jesus Christ is revealed to the whole world (1 Peter 1:3-7, NLT).

Amen!

By Karen E. Connell

IF POSSIBLE...Even the Very Elect Will Be Deceived
Many professing Christians are following ministers and ministries simply because they operate in signs and wonders. It is important to know what the Bible has to say about the subject of deception that Jesus said would be rampant in the end times in which we are living. Multitudes are falling prey to seducing spirits and doctrines of demons. In this book Karen is sounding the alarm with the hope that those who have ears will hear. This book is a must read for those who desire more than "milk" and are hungry for real "meat" from God's word.
295 pages

Investigating and Experiencing... The Glory of God
This booklet is adapted from the *book IF POSSIBLE...Even the Very Elect Will Be Deceived*. This study is a biblical perspective on a most important but often misunderstood subject known as "The Glory of God." The true Glory of God is the key to true revival!
68 pages

Spiritual Warfare... A Biblical Perspective
There is much being taught and written on the subject of *spiritual warfare* within many Christian circles. For over forty years Karen has personally been involved in several Christian movements, namely the Pentecostal, Charismatic and most recently the New Apostolic Reformation (NAR) movements, all of which teach and practice some form of spiritual warfare. In this book she shares some of what God has revealed to her through His Word concerning some of the errors and excesses that are occurring.
61 pages

Content No Matter What!
Is it possible to be content not matter what? Karen reveals how she leaned that we can choose to be BLESSED or STRESSED! This is the first in the *OVERCOMERS SERIES* of mini booklets. Karen Connell shares a Biblical perspective on many important issues so God's people can be overcomer's and not overcome by their life's circumstances.
30 pages

Spiritual Gifts Manual 213 pages

Equipping the saints for the work of their ministry!

Enroll now in our FREE On Line or correspondence
Spiritual Gifts Course
This Spiritual Gifts Manual covers such subjects as:

- The different categories of gifts and their purpose

- How to identify the true operation and motivation for God's gifts.

- Identifying your spiritual gifts—and how to receive the gifts needed for your calling in the "work of your ministry"

All on-line students receive at no charge...

- The *Spiritual Gifts Manual* Through the mail or PDF on-line download

- Access to companion teachings by mp3 downloads or CD's by mail

- If preferred students can also take the course as a mail correspondence course

Upon finishing the course a *Certificate of Completion*
will be awarded to the student.

Three Fold Cord Healing and Deliverance Manual & Teaching CD's
225 pages

Professing Christians often struggle with things like anger, insecurity and worth issues simply because they lack healing and deliverance in all areas of their being, (body soul and spirit). The Biblical principle of the *three fold cord* states *"...a three fold cord is not easily broken"* Eccl 4:12 This Manual and 24 CD companion teaching series, reveals how the three fold cord of *rejection—bitterness—pride* are the foundation for many physical, physiological and spiritual problems. Karen Connell shares key Biblical truths given to her by God during years of seeking His word for answers to her own struggles as a Christian; because of the physical, emotional and sexual abuse experienced in her own life. What Karen shares in this manual is the result of her *healing*, *deliverance* and *victory* over compulsive and addictive behavior, rooted in insecurity, anger and fear coming from the forces of darkness. Ministers and Christians in all walks of life have found victory through this material. You can too!

Please complete this form to place an order by mail... For more resources by Karen Connell go to: **www.extendedlife.net** resource page

Name_____

Address_____

City_____State_____Zip_____

Phone (   )_____e-mail_____

I have enclosed a love offering in the amount of $_____

- Please check if you would like to be placed on our mailing list... *(You may also include names and addresses of others that may also desire a copy).*

How many FREE copies of the following you would like?

___Copies of the *Extended Life C.T.M.* **Resource Catalog**

___Copies of the **Trumpet Sounds Volume #1 Booklet**

___Copies of: Current **Trumpet Sounds Newsletter**

___Copies of other resources listed below:

_____
_____
_____
_____

There is **no charge** for these products or for our newsletter. Any offering to help with production and mailing costs is always very much appreciated!
Checks may be made payable to:
Extended Life CTM
734 W. Water St. Hancock, MI 49930
Phone: (906) 482-6467

Made in the USA
San Bernardino, CA
05 September 2016